28 Day Financial Renaissance

28 Day Financial Renaissance

Osiola Henderson

McKinney, Texas, USA

ISBN 1450546595
LCCN

Printed in the United States of America.

Microsoft Office and Microsoft Excel are registered trademarks of Microsoft. Apple and the iPhone are registered trademarks of Apple Corporation. Sony and BluRay, Yahoo, Google, MSN, MSNBC, CNN, Dow Jones and the Dow Jones Industrial Average, Standard and Poor's and the S&P 500, the Chicago Board Options Exchange, the *Wall Street Journal*, Merriam-Webster, McDonald's, Jack in the Box, Mr. Gatti's Pizza, American Idol, Wal-Mart, Exxon, Belo, W. R. Grace, Del Monte, Cintas, Buffalo Wild Wings, Ethan Allen Interiors, Independent Bank, and the Grocery Game are registered trademarks of their parent companies and/or owners.

Any reference in this text to the aforementioned entities is for informational purposes only and does not constitute any relationship with the companies, their websites, or their businesses.

This book is designed to provide a brief introduction regarding the subjects discussed. It is sold with the understanding that there is no specific advice contained herein. Nothing in this text should be considered as the basis for any investment, tax or insurance program. Please consult your financial adviser, insurance professional, and tax adviser for specific advice in the areas mentioned above.

A good man leaves an inheritance for his children's children.

Proverbs 13:22

Contents

Preface

As a child, I was told that it takes forty days to break a habit or to create a new one. During a class I took as an adult, I was surprised to learn that number was now down to twenty-eight days. If you have the commitment, then you are only twenty-eight days from a new and better you. Remember the caveat, however—don't skip any days, or you must start over.

My goal is to help you change your financial position in life during the next twenty-eight days. It doesn't really matter your current financial position; my goal is to help you improve with what you have and to help you become more aware of things that may be standing in your way.

I make no promises that you will miraculously become wealthy. What I will present to you is a group of concepts, activities, and ideas that can make you financially stable. My intent is not to bore or bog you down with too many technical details, but to give you a read that is easy to understand yet educational. The end result will be up to you and your imagination. I hope that by the end of the month, you will be full of enthusiasm and that you will finally regain control of your financial life.

Understand one thing, though: managing your finances can be fun and exciting, but it can also be a chore, especially if you are overly burdened with expenses and a lack of income. What you will need is commitment, discipline, and determination.

Your commitment will be tested every day by your desire to put off getting started or by your procrastination in completing the tasks of the day. Keep a positive attitude as you complete the activities. Your efforts will be rewarded at the end of the process. My suggestion to you is that you pick a start date, tell someone what you are doing, and then jump right in. Don't listen to any negatives that you might hear about why you shouldn't being trying to improve your finances. Think positively and mark your calendar, because for the next month you will be doing something that will help yourself, your family, and possibly even your community.

Discipline will be required, as you will be tempted to cheat or to take shortcuts, maybe even the easy route. Some of the activities you will do will require you to do things a certain way. Some may require a bit of time or effort, but keep in mind that the end result is what you are working on, not your day-to-day operations. Remember that anything worth having requires some sort of work.

Your determination will let you know how successful you will be at the end of this project. You can embrace the changes, become excited about the opportunity, and really make a difference in your life, or you can stand by and just let life keep happening to you. Your determination will be like the wood that you place on a fire, fueling your actions from day to day and pulling you to higher heights. Just as the runner knows that at mile twenty-six he or she is almost there, your determination will fuel you toward the last steps and on to victory.

If it sounds like you will be in training for some type of sporting event, then you can think of it that way. The you that would like to make a change in your financial life is competing with the you that is currently in the position you are in—unhappy and wishing for a breakthrough.

Let me caution you that there will be peaks and valleys. You will have joys and pains. You may even experience a bit of frustration with the whole process, but your commitment to achievement, your discipline in staying on task, and your determination to seeing this through to the end will help you to complete the project.

This book is meant to help you to build successful financial habits. Be sure to write all over the pages as the "aha" moments pop up. The process that you will go through over the next twenty-eight days will eventually become etched into your mind and be as natural for you as brushing your teeth or driving a car. This process will never be complete; it will always need to be tweaked, worked with, and continually under review. After you have finished the exercises in this book, however, you will be equipped for everything that comes your way.

The first step is always the hardest, and the first step is admitting that you have a problem. The exercises in this book are meant to help you make permanent changes to your finances. Simply by purchasing this book, you have taken that first step.

Acknowledgments

I would like to take a moment to thank some really important people for helping to complete this project. First, I would like to thank Jennifer Lehmberg, my neighbor and friend and a truly gifted graphic designer, for helping me with my cover along with other projects over the years. I would also like to thank Sally I. Steele for helping me to correct my writing mistakes and for editing this work and making it ready for you to read.

From the beginning, I have had some great women influencing my life. My mother, Katherine, always encourages me to achieve the best and never settle for good enough. Her wisdom is greater than her years, and the financial hurdles she has overcome have really made her a leader in the community when it comes to money. My mother forges ahead against all odds and the people she encounters are better for the time they spent with her. It doesn't take long for you to realize that she is a God-fearing woman. She simply tries to make a way for her children first, and then for herself. Along the way, she has really taught me some valuable life lessons.

My grandmothers, Beatrice and Ideller, who from the time I was born prayed for me and my success, taught me respect, how to value life, and most importantly, how to not count on tomorrow. I can still hear my great-grandmother, Ideller, as she would say, "Gods willing, I will do this tomorrow." She knew that today was a gift and tomorrow was not promised.

My daughter, Briauna, who looks up to me for every answer but more importantly loves to talk about money and business, has a passion and drive that will help her to achieve great heights. Even at her young age, she is a gifted marketer. She is truly gifted and I am looking forward to watching her blossom into the woman that God wants her to be.

My wife, Valencia, who started me on the quest to write simply by buying me a journal and a pen and telling me to put some thoughts to paper, is my biggest encourager. Our conversations are always centered on how to improve our community and how to make day-to-day life mean more than just paying bills and buying stuff. Together we are working on building a legacy.

My newest inspiration is my newborn son, Isaiah. He has inspired me to surpass all of my self-imposed limits and to expect more out of life. His smile gives me the energy to move to new levels.

I would also say thank you to two teachers, Mr. Echols from Nimitz High School, and Mrs. Jordan from C. E. King High School, who opened my eyes to want to write, even though at the time I didn't have the ability yet.

And thank you for making this purchase. I hope that you are able to learn a lot from the words contained within these pages. I encourage you to make this a stepping stone to what should be the joy of managing your money.

Unit 1: Preplanning

1

Psychology of Money

Before you begin, you will have to work on your mental attitude about money. This is important because how you think about your money will ultimately determine how you will treat your money.

Most of your attitudes about money can be attributed to how money was treated when you were growing up. Think back to when you were a child and picture how your mother dealt with money, and then picture how your father dealt with money. Answer the following questions:

- Was your mother a saver and your father a spender?
- Did your father work hard to save while your mother chose to go shopping?
- Did your family have any discussions about while you were growing up?
- Was money in short supply?
- What financial challenges do you remember having as a child?
- What lessons did you learn about money as a child?

Now that you have answered those questions, ask yourself how you now treat your money. You will probably notice some similarities between how you treat money and how your parents treated money.

For instance, if money was abundant in your home when you were a child, then you may now be a shopper and a spender.

The abundance of resources might have taught you that money will always be there as long as you work for it. You may feel that you are free to buy what you would like as soon as you want it.

On the other hand, you may have grown up in a home where money was in short supply. In this case, you might have gone in one of two directions.

The first direction is that of being a saver, because as a child you seemed to never have enough. You may be determined to never be in that position again. Conversely, you may have gravitated to the other end of the spectrum by becoming a spender. Since you were never able to have everything that you wanted as a child, you may now be committed to fulfilling even your smallest whims.

Lastly, were both of your parents savers? Did they teach you the value of a dollar? Did they teach you to respect money and to make sure that you have enough to provide for yourself and to cover emergencies that may occur in the future?

Now that you've examined your relationship with money, you can begin to understand why you do some of the things that you do. You may really understand some of your past financial mistakes. You may also now recognize why it is so hard for you to reduce your debts, to save for your future, or even to stockpile money for a rainy day.

You can use this knowledge to help mold yourself into the new you who will do everything in balance. You can save and accumulate at the same time and still live the lifestyle that you would like to have.

Shopping

Human nature is such that we all love to shop. The desire seems to be wired within us. Shopping elicits an emotional response that causes endorphins to be released into the bloodstream—the same endorphins that are released during sex. No wonder shopping is addictive!

Spending allows us to feel good about ourselves, our situations, and our families at a time when nothing else is going well. The fact that shopping produces an emotional response is the very reason that it is so dangerous. By allowing themselves to be overcome with trying to stay happy all the time, many people have ruined their financial lives as well as their families.

Have you ever noticed someone who was constantly overspending and wondered how or why they were doing it? If you were to ask them, I bet you would discover some deep feeling of sorrow or unease. For them, shopping is a crutch, or better termed, a temporary escape from the reality of life.

To be successful financially, we must overcome the day-to-day urges to shop uncontrollably. We have to give ourselves a set of guidelines that can help us stay on track. Like our government, we need a system of checks and balances that will help us during our times of weakness, especially after an emotional letdown. For some of us, that means creating our own risk and reward system.

Look around the stores during the holiday shopping season and notice the smiles on people's faces. Their glow can be seen across a room. But while their smiles are big, their shopping carts are fuller than originally hoped for. The reason for this generosity is twofold; we love to shop, and we love for people to think highly of us.

About two months later, once bills come due, the predominant look upon faces is not one of adoration, but of disbelief—disbelief that, yet again, we shopped well past our limits and will now spend the remainder of the year paying off these thoughtful gestures.

When shopping, you have to set up limits; how much will you spend this year? What is your price per gift? If you spend too much on one gift, then who gets a smaller gift so that you can stay on track? You may be thinking that you can go overboard because the holidays are here, but the holidays, along with vacations, are when you should be your strictest. Would these occasions not be as joyous with less expensive gifts?

With these temptations in mind, how can you protect your financial goals and stay on track?

First, list your shopping in your spending plan (discussed in greater detail in Chapter 12). You created it so that you would know how much money each category should have. Furthermore, you should have been planning for all of your purchases throughout the year and should now have most of your shopping funds accumulated and ready to spend.

Second, recognize your limits and stick to them. When the pot is empty, it is time to go home. There should be no wiggle room for purchases that you have not planned out previously. Discipline and commitment are tested during times when shopping comes into play.

Third, shop from a list. If it is important enough to buy, then it should be important enough for you to write down. If you see something that you do not need and it is not on your list, leave it there until such a time that you remember to put it on your shopping list. By using a list, you protect yourself from those impulse buys that the stores count on you making.

Shopping from a list also gives you the opportunity to take advantage of one other cost-saving measure—coupons. If you know in advance what you are purchasing, you can look for sales and make your purchases where you will get the lowest prices while taking advantage of coupons that save you money. After a short while, you will begin to recognize the best days and stores for making purchases. In terms of groceries, you may be able to take advantage of doubling or tripling savings from manufacturers' coupons.

Fourth, never purchase items as soon as they come out. Stores love shoppers who follow trends and feed on their need to be the first one to have Item X. What you may not realize is that most times, the prices come down after a couple of weeks and those who waited get a better deal. So what if you got the first one?

Trends are set because of advertising hype and the surge of people buying something that they ordinarily would not have purchased; leave the next big thing on the shelf and settle for the old reliable. Most trends are aimed at men who love gadgets, teens who love bright colors, or women who love shoes. If you can wait until the initial rush has passed, you can save yourself a lot of money. BluRay players, for example, debuted at over $300, and now the players are down to $120. The newer players are faster, smaller, and have more features. The same thing happened with the rollout of Apple's iPhone. The newer version had fewer bugs and cost a mere third of the original. Can you recall a time when you purchased an item, only to be disappointed later when your friend told you what they paid for the same item?

Stores place items on clearance and offer deep discounts not because these items failed to sell initially, but because the stores need to turn over their inventory for the next big thing. When they do, you have an opportunity to maximize your shopping dollar. You just need to be patient. You can buy summer clothes in the winter and winter clothes in the summer, athletic gear out of season, and even cars at deep discounts if you are willing to sacrifice having current fashions today.

Fifth, for any item that you have not planned to purchase but feel you must have, write down the information pertaining to it (cost, store location, description), take the information home, and place it on your refrigerator for two weeks. If, after the two week cool-down period, you feel that you must have the item and you can afford it without using credit, then go ahead and make the purchase. If you cannot justify the purchase after the two week cool-down, then you probably didn't need it anyway—just look around your kitchen or garage for examples of must-have items that you either never used or didn't realize that you had.

Lastly, never purchase anything when you are extremely happy, excited, upset, or otherwise outside your normal emotional disposition, because you are more likely to make a financial mistake. Some mistakes can be corrected, while others are final. If you are a spender and feel that you must make a purchase, contact someone you trust who can help you overcome the urge. By doing something else that you enjoy, you can exchange one emotional boost for another.

All for One and One for All

Success is not always final and failure is not always certain.
—Winston Churchill

While your past mistakes do not condemn you, your current position is never a certainty. You cannot take for granted your past successes and blindly assume that they will continue to occur. The one thing that we know for certain is that uncertainty will prevail. Life itself is unpredictable, and just when you think everything is perfect, your life will shift.

Just as it was in ancient times, today it is hard to change your position in society. What you will be attempting to do is very difficult, very frustrating, and can be a bit paralyzing. If it were easy, the vast majority of Americans would already be financially responsible, financially aware, and on the road to financial independence. Instead, few Americans are on that path.

To experience your breakthrough, you, your spouse, and your children will have to stay on track and follow the plan. It is impossible to row a boat if the person in the front and the person in the back are paddling in different directions. Before you begin to make any changes, make sure that you are in agreement with your significant other. Do yourself a favor and make sure that each person involved is doing his or her part in order to reach your goal.

This means that a bad day is not an excuse to go out and buy a new big flat-screen television. It also means that no new purse and shoe combinations can appear on a Saturday night after a rough week at work.

As long as you and your family agree to participate and go down the same path, rest assured that you will be making some great strides in your financial life. After all, no one ever said that where you are today has to be where you will be tomorrow. Each day is another opportunity to do something positive in your life.

Pay Yourself First

The expression "pay yourself first" just makes sense—shouldn't you want to put some funds back for yourself? You work hard every day for your money, wait all week to collect the small amount that you have traded your time for, and then spend all that you earn on bills and expenses. Finally, after everything else has been paid for, you then try to put some of it back for tomorrow.

As a society, we save less than 1% of our earnings on an annual basis. This trend is not just happening within the lower income households, but is also happening throughout the country and includes approximately 90% of Americans. That's right—90% of Americans, citizens of the wealthiest country in the world, save less than one dollar for every hundred dollars we earn!

Our debts are skyrocketing, and it is no wonder that our financial markets are in turmoil; we finance everything from our educations to our healthcare and investments. We borrow too much and own too little. We try to live on more while earning less. For these reasons, paying yourself first is such a critical concept.

Before the Twin Towers were hit in New York on September 11, 2001, our economy was at the peak of a wealth explosion. It was a mortgaged wealth, but was wealth nonetheless.

The wealth was mortgaged because the holdings in many investors' accounts were purchased using a margin account, which allows the investor to use credit extended by the broker-dealer to purchase securities. When the value of the holding in the margin account falls below a certain level, the broker-dealer will issue what is called a margin call. This margin call is a request for the investor to deposit more money in the account to cover the minimum asset-to-loan ratio in the margin account.

As the stock market continued its decline, broker-dealers had to issue multiple margin calls. Cash-strapped investors sold assets in retirement accounts, sold vehicles, and even took out second mortgages to cover the request for more cash. This was one reason that the stock market continued to fall.

As a result of the market decline, we entered a very deep recession. Fear of another terrorist attack and a struggling economy caused many Americans to nest, to focus on their homes, and to spend time away from public areas. Home improvement boomed while consumer spending in restaurants, travel, and entertainment began to wane. President George W. Bush tried various ways of stimulating the economy, which included issuing tax stimulus checks to encourage consumers to spend more and kick-start the economy.

For a short time it seemed to work, but unfortunately, consumers could only help the economy with a little push due to their shrinking incomes. Conversely, corporations that up until the attacks had been overspending began to stockpile money at an alarming rate. All of a sudden it was no longer prudent for corporate officials to reinvest and expand their businesses; instead, they chose to build up their cash reserves to protect themselves in case the credit markets failed. These corporate officials refused to spend or to rehire laid-off workers, even though the economy showed signs of improvement. They elected to not replace aging equipment. They instead chose to build up large stockpiles of money to make their balance sheets look good. Some of these reserves equaled more than $35 billion in cash, an unprecedented amount for corporations.

Consumers were asked repeatedly on news channels and by presidential addresses to spend, and not save. They were even encouraged to not save the stimulus checks, even though layoffs were widespread. Consumers were asked to save the economy, to keep the country afloat until corporate spending returned. Consumers complied with ballooning debts, while corporate executives received huge bonuses. To make matters worse, when companies began spending again, it was to purchase other corporations so that they could lay off additional workers to fix problems in their financial statements that were not disclosed during previous filings.

The economy did improve after 2001, but it began to take another downturn due to legislative changes related to the credit minimum payments along with more stringent rules related to bankruptcy. Additionally, exotic mortgage products, such as interest-only loans and adjustable-rate mortgages, caused financial markets to tumble. Executives of some corporations were forced to beg the government for a bailout. Some of the largest financial institutions failed, and credit and lending froze, leaving not only the American economy in a tailspin, but also affecting markets around the world. To solve the problem, the government began to lend funds to corporations and financial institutions that were deemed too large to fail in order to revive them and give company officials time to clean up their acts. In return for the assistance, some corporations immediately issued bonuses to their executives. Many companies began to impose greater fees on the consumers they were now relying on to stay in business.

And so, within ten years, the American consumer has been responsible for salvaging the economy twice. Now, when it is the consumers' turn to get a bailout, they are instead turned away by financial institutions and told that no aid is available. Hearing this from banks that our tax dollars just bailed out not only angers Americans, but is also the perfect reason why we need to save for ourselves and to prepare our households for the rainy days ahead. It is also a reason why no corporation should ever again be considered too big to fail.

Paying yourself first means taking at least 10% of your income and putting it away as soon as you earn it. This money is placed aside before any other payments are made. The goal is to place these funds in an account and forget about them. By doing so, you will have protected yourself for when the next bubble bursts. The next time you will be prepared for the unexpected.

Paying yourself first involves knowing that you are not working just to pay your bills, but instead are doing something for yourself and your family. You are protecting your own household. Paying yourself first is creating your own bailout plan. You will be creating your own cushion, just as corporations have done for the past eight years, and you will be preparing a more secure future for your family.

Taking 10% of your income and putting it away can be a challenge, especially with all the expenses you have become accustomed to. I attest that you must make the sacrifice. You must make the changes necessary to ensure that it is possible. I understand that for some of you, it will mean running your household on 80% rather than 90% due to your religious and charitable contributions. I contend that it is possible, and that if you start and stick to the plan for three months, soon you will not even miss the funds. You will, however, begin to notice an increase in how much your attitude changes toward money. How much better would you feel if you knew that you were not spending every dollar you earned?

Add a bill with your name on it, place the entry in your financial software, Excel spreadsheet, or whatever method you use to track your bills, and begin to pay yourself. If it helps you, place a due date on the bill that matches your pay dates and mail yourself a bill. Do whatever it takes to get your household on the right financial track.

Make saving fun by paying the amount you are putting aside in an account that you don't use. Make collection calls and send emails to yourself to make sure that you pay yourself. You will begin to build your account one paycheck at a time. Soon you will realize the compounding effect of paying yourself first.

Create your own enthusiasm, stick to the plan, and you will notice your happiness grow. You deserve to reap some fruits from the labors of the week. Not one person is going to take care of you the way that you will take care of yourself in the event of an emergency, so stockpile your own reserves for the coming trouble. You can then rest, knowing that you are prepared for the financial challenges that may come or that may be created by legislative changes.

Don't wait for a new year or your next raise to come through before you get started. Dive right in today by placing a call to your human resources department to obtain a payroll change form. If you have to, call your bank and change your deposits. Put this book down and do it now, if possible, while the urge is strong. Carpe diem!

Unit 2: Credit

Credit

Let us now turn our attention to credit and the many uses, benefits, and dangers of using it. For the majority of us, life would not exist without having credit. Our homes, our cars, our businesses, and even our educations are financed using credit. A large portion of the investments on Wall Street are made using **credit**, otherwise known as **margin**.

Shall we look back at some of the ways that credit began? The farmer who wanted to plant crops would often go to the banker to borrow money until the harvest came in. Once the harvest came in, the farmer would sell his goods, collect his profit, repay his debts, and purchase equipment for the next year. This process has continued on to become the foundation for this country.

Today, when a businessman has a great idea, he will go to a bank, fill out some forms, present a business plan, and then borrow money to fund his project. The businessman will sell his goods and then collect his profits. With the extra money, he will, in turn, repay his debts and hire employees. Those employees work for wages and salaries. These wages would help the employees fulfill their lives with their wants and desires. This process is what we call commerce.

This creation of commerce and also the creation of business has led us to different spots in society. We now have those who have money and nice things and those who aspire to have money and who want nice things. That constant push, an urge to have more, to do more, and to be more than what we are right now is what gets most of us into trouble with credit. It all starts with the declaration, "I'll fill out an application to get this credit card. I will only use it in the event of an emergency." Then we go to the mall, get caught up in all of the excitement, and lose control.

No one ever says that they want to be in debt. We do, however, get caught up in the emotion that rushes into us by purchasing new items. After all, we all want "stuff," and with the abundance of "stuff" that is available, we become discontent in our own lives.

The problem starts just after you arrive at a friend's home and notice their new possessions and ask yourself, why not me? No longer are you content with saving your money for the next year. You begin to think that it's okay to buy this today and pay for it on Friday when your check comes in.

Remember that life is what happens in between what you plan and what you get. Friday arrives and all of a sudden something else has come up that requires the money you were planning on sending to the credit card company. So what do you do?

You begin to justify not making the payment. You take care of today's emergency and go about your life unhappily, still not content with what you have or where you are, and the cycle continues.

But it doesn't stop there; it would probably be okay if you only used the card for one or two small purchases, but instead you max out the first credit card, and then you max out the second credit card, and sometimes, if you're a real overachiever, you max out card number ten.

Keep in mind, though, that getting into debt is a process. It does not happen overnight—you do not accumulate all the purchases overnight, nor will you resolve the problem overnight. This process continues until you can change your behavior and your attitude.

After all, we want what we want, and we want it now!

Credit

We want nice homes, we want nice cars, we want to be admired for ourselves, for our appearances, and for our positions in society. We also want to feel the joy of receiving compliments that comes from owning nice things.

The reason that we do what we do and the reason that we have the debts that we have is all related to an emotion, the same one that originates in the pleasure center of the brain and is stimulated by sex and drugs. This emotion is the reason that we have anonymous groups for sex, drugs, and also for shopping.

So is credit bad? No, the improper use and management of credit is what causes problems. Although we learn a lot of things in school, we never, unfortunately, learn money management. To our detriment, we've never learned how to properly manage our finances or our credit.

You may disagree and believe that our parents should have taught us those lessons about money. But who would have taught them?

We've been taught how to cook, how to drive, how to sew, and how to be respectful, but when it comes to money, no one ever wants to teach us lessons until after we've made mistakes. Why is that? What is so wrong with our society that a generation is not taught at an early age how to take care of their money?

It is no secret that banks don't want a financially responsible generation because it would hurt their profits. If everyone knew how to take care of their money, then banks would surely lose their big buildings downtown.

To credit card companies, there are two types of individuals: deadbeats and revolvers. If there was ever a time when you would want to be called a deadbeat, it is when the conversation is centered on your use of credit; **deadbeats** are those cardholders who pay their balances in full each month. Credit card companies make no money off of these customers, and so the companies must try different ways of enticing deadbeats to carry a monthly balance. Deadbeats make up a small portion of cardholders. Oftentimes these credit card holders choose cards with no annual or application fees. Some of these cardholders use credit cards for each of their expenses throughout the month and then send in one check to cover the entire balance. Other deadbeats simply collect open cards in an effort to keep a high credit score. Their accounts are rarely used and have no balances except for the one or two transactions that are placed on the account annually to keep them open.

Conversely, **revolvers** are the bread and butter of credit card companies' balance sheets. These cardholders carry monthly balances on their accounts, never look at the small print, and become trapped by fees and minimum payments into long-term relationships with their credit card companies.

If you look at your credit card statements, you may discover that many of your purchases were small. The real challenge is in locating the merchandise that you purchased long ago but are still making payments toward.

To be fair, I understand that for some of us, using credit allows us to bridge the gap between our monthly expenses and our monthly income. Circumstances change and may severely impact your lifestyle. In this economic climate, it is no surprise that debts are on the rise, incomes are falling, and bankruptcies and foreclosures have become commonplace.

For some people, this is understandable. These are the people who have suffered from legislative changes in credit laws, which caused their payments to double. These are the people who purchased sport utility vehicles and now try to keep gas in them at $4.50 per gallon. These are the people who were recently laid off and had no choice but to use credit to make ends meet. This group of the population may be justified in their use of credit.

But then there are others who are in debt simply because of their own greed, lack of discipline, or lack of ambition. Sometimes they are shopaholics, while other times they are simply trying to keep up with the Joneses. Often their attitude is that they must have the same item as someone else, and they must have it now, because no one is going to outclass them.

These individuals are very dangerous to themselves financially, and will oftentimes be in debt for long periods of time. Usually they are not waiting on a financial breakthrough; they are waiting on their next paycheck to come in so they can make yet another purchase.

Which category best describes your situation?

1	My financial situation has changed due to a change in income or loss of employment.
2	My financial situation has been impacted by an unexpected expense.
3	I like making purchases and feel that because I work hard, I am entitled to them whenever I see fit.
4	They gave me the card, and I'm going to use it.

If you fall into category one or two, you will find it easier to follow the debt reduction schedule than will those in categories three or four. It is those in the latter two groups who will find it restrictive, the reason being that they are used to making purchases whenever, wherever, and with whatever means available.

Where do you begin to make the changes that will help you minimize your debts? Begin by first gathering all of your credit cards and credit card statements. Create a table that looks like Table 1, listing all of your debts, the charged interest rate, the due date, the payment required, and the actual payment submitted. You may find it helpful to create this table in Microsoft Excel or a similar spreadsheet program, as it will allow you to manipulate the data more easily.

Creditor	Balance	Interest Rate	Due Date	Amount Due	Payment Made
Always Bank	$5,000	12.99%	5th	$200	$225
Forever Bank	$10,000	7.9%	10th	$400	$400
Ideal Bank	$8,300	15.99%	18th	$332	$350
Utopia Bank	$900	21.99%	7th	$36	$50

Table 1: Creditor Listing

Now that you have created the table, your goal is to fill it in and create a plan to repay the debts that burden you on a monthly basis.

To start, place your credit card statements in order from highest interest rate to lowest interest rate. Begin filling in the table, beginning with the highest interest rate first and ending with the lowest interest rate.

Be sure to fill in as much information as you can, including the due dates and payment amounts.

If you make any additional payments or send additional funds, such as $10 extra per month, then enter the actual payment that you make each month into the "Payment Made" column. You'll use this information to figure out how to repay your credit cards. Refer to Kelly Borrower's example below to see how to proceed. Each of Kelly's creditors require a 4% minimum monthly payment.

Credit

Creditor	Balance	Interest Rate	Due Date	Amount Due	Payment Made
Utopia Bank	$900	21.99%	7th	$36	$50
Ideal Bank	$8,300	15.99%	18th	$332	$350
Always Bank	$5,000	12.99%	5th	$200	$225
Forever Bank	$10,000	7.9%	10th	$400	$400

Table 2: Creditor Listing with Interest Rates Highest to Lowest

As you can see in Table 2, the highest interest rate in this example belongs to the Utopia Bank credit card. Also notice that in this example, Kelly is paying extra every month towards the balance on each card, just like her parents told her to do. She is only required to pay $968 per month total to all of her credit cards, but is currently paying $1025. The difference in the amount due and the amount that she is currently paying is $57. Unfortunately, Kelly is just not getting out of debt fast enough. The $57 can be used more wisely.

For this example, let's assume that after creating her budget and mapping out all of her expenses, Kelly has $100 extra per month that she can commit to her debts. This additional $100, along with the $57 that the Kelly is already sending to the creditors, will be used as the first step to repaying the debt on the Utopia Bank credit card.

To get out of debt faster, Kelly will pay the minimums on all of the cards except for Utopia Bank's card, which will receive the additional $157 per month until the debt is repaid. In this example, Utopia Bank's credit card will be repaid in five months, using the monthly payment of $193, which includes the required $36 plus the additional $157 (the $100 committed from her budget and the extra $57 that she had been sending to her creditors).

At the end of the five months, Kelly will turn her attention to Ideal Bank and begin to accelerate the repayment of the debt; instead of only submitting the extra $157, she will send the entire $193 (which includes the $36 that was being sent to Utopia Bank's credit card plus the additional $157) to Ideal Bank, along with the required minimum payment of $332. At $525 per month, Ideal Bank's balance will begin to decline quickly. Kelly will make minimum payments on all remaining credit cards until Ideal Bank has a balance of zero.

Once Ideal Bank is repaid, Kelly now has $525 extra to use to repay Always Bank. Since Kelly has been on the program for a while, she clearly has an understanding of the process. Kelly now knows that she will be sending $725 to Always Bank until she has this debt repaid, while at the same time paying the monthly minimum to Forever Bank. Soon, Always Bank will no longer hold a debt over the head of our very smart borrower and the last card on the list will begin to be repaid.

Forever Bank will be the last card to be repaid because it had the lowest interest rate. Of all of the cards Kelly had, this card cost her the least in terms of interest monthly. Repaying Forever Bank will be very fast because Kelly now has $1125 per month to send in repayment of the debt. Also keep in mind that she has been making some progress in satisfying the debt by making minimum payments while the repayment plan was focused on the other credit cards.

Now that all of the credit cards are repaid, Kelly can sleep happily, knowing that she is debt free. Moreover, Kelly now has demonstrated an ability to save and to stick to a dedicated plan of action. What is more amazing is that Kelly now has $1125 per month that she is not accustomed to having that can be used to fund retirement accounts, to build up cash reserves, and to make investments and other income-producing opportunities.

The worse thing for Kelly to do would be to celebrate by going out to shop. Mentally, she is not used to having these funds and should continue to manage her finances as if the money did not exist. The funds can instead be diverted into accounts that will generate income for Kelly.

One of the first things Kelly should do after all of the accounts have been repaid is to build an emergency fund. By having an emergency fund, she can ensure that her financial train doesn't get derailed just as it is leaving the station.

Now that you know how the repayment plan works, create one for your specific situation and begin the repayment process next month. Refer to your plan monthly and use it as visual proof of the progress that you are making.

Once you pay off your credit cards, you can either close them or choose to operate as a deadbeat, keeping your accounts open but not using them.

As you pay off your credit cards, grab a pair of scissors and cut them up, or stick them in a jar of water and place the jar in your freezer.

Payday Loans

If you listen to the radio or watch a lot of late-night commercials on television, you'll notice that there's been an increase in the number of payday loan advertisements. It is no wonder that during these economic times, these companies are gaining popularity. Banks are rejecting borrowers at an alarming rate. Companies are laying off employees, lowering their salaries, and shutting their doors for weeks at a time to try to save money. Unfortunately for Joe Consumer, whose lifestyle has come to rely on his usual pay scale, the company's money-saving efforts actually hurt his financial situation.

In addition to the cuts being made at the company level, creditors are also closing credit lines, increasing minimum payments, and charging more fees. Joe Consumer needs to figure out a way to make ends meet. The only way that he knows to stay afloat is to borrow money. Unfortunately for him, the only credit available is through these payday loan corporations. The process begins simply, with one loan, minimal monthly payments, and the expectation that things will get better as the months go on. For most people, a single loan is enough to get out of trouble and back onto the right track financially.

For others, the ease of getting the money and the speed at which it becomes available to them is too enticing to handle. They take out a second loan and the money from that loan is used to pay for the first loan. A third loan becomes necessary to pay for the second loan, and the process spirals out of control. I've seen people with seven or eight of these loans, each of which is being used to pay for a previous loan that had been used to finance unimportant purchases. Necessity has been replaced with greed as obtaining money requires only a phone call.

When you borrow these funds, you relinquish your routing numbers, your checking account information, and also your payroll information. The form you sign authorizes your payday loan company to draft out payments in the event of a delinquency from your bank or paycheck.

These companies don't really care that your mortgage is due or that you're late with your car payment; their sole concern is that you promised to pay them on a particular day. When you are late on your payments, you are forced to take out another payday loan.

If you find yourself in financial trouble, don't go to credit counseling services, because they have all the information they need to go into your account at any time and withdraw money.

High interest rates, frontloaded interest, and an all-access pass to your banking account make these loans very dangerous; stay away from them at all costs. At some point, you may have to use one of these loans to pay for an unexpected repair, but if you do so, it is very important that you repay the account and close it as soon as possible. You do not want to fall into the trap of revolving payday loans.

Credit Without Credit

"I pay off everything I purchase each month and don't carry a balance on my credit card," one man boasted. While trying to purchase a vehicle, though, he learned that he either would need a huge down payment or would need to obtain a cosigner to assist him in making his first purchase. He didn't understand why he didn't have excellent credit; he had made all his payments in full each month ever since his parents helped him to get the card at age seventeen.

This man's parents taught him correctly; he *should* pay all his credit bills by the end of the month. Unfortunately, the lesson about carrying a small balance on the cards to help create a payment history was left out. Payment history is what creditors use to assign a credit score. To his creditors, he was a payer, but to the industry, he was considered a deadbeat.

He had built no history of making payments and had not proven that he could make regular payments on accounts that report to any of the major credit reporting agencies (TransUnion, Experian, and Equifax).

The majority of creditors report the payment history of all their account holders to the reporting agencies once a month. If an account has a zero balance at one reporting and has a zero balance at the next reporting, then there is nothing to report for that period. Essentially, the account holder has no activity on the card, so the account will not reflect any of the charges made during the course of the billing cycle.

This man is at least lucky that he has a credit card already. All he would have to do to have a good payment history is make a purchase and carry the balance for six months to a year and then pay off the debt. Six months may not be long enough, as reporting agencies would then classify the borrower as having new credit or being too new to rate. The borrower would still find difficulty in obtaining some loans or lines of credit.

A solid credit history with at least two years of payments should be sufficient to allow the borrower to possess a good credit score. The amount of the purchases is not important; the timely payment history is what is necessary to create the high credit score.

One way to build a solid history is to obtain a loan at your local bank. Use the proceeds from the loan to purchase a **certificate of deposit, or CD,** with the same term as the loan. Make monthly payments on the loan, and at the end of the term, cash in the CD. Depending on the interest rates of the loan and the CD, you will find yourself only out a small amount of money, equaling the difference between the cost of the interest paid on the loan and the interest earned on the CD. A solid payment history will be recorded and you will also have some money in savings.

Another way to build credit is to obtain a **secured credit card** from your local bank. A secured credit card is easy to obtain because you deposit money in an account that is linked to the credit card. The deposit is used to guarantee the borrower's repayment on the credit card. Should the borrower default on repayment, the lender would simply cash in the deposit and deactivate the credit card. The amount of the credit line is customarily equal to the amount of the deposit in the account.

Most of the deposit accounts associated with secured credit cards earn a small amount of interest while the account is in use. Don't concentrate on the interest you will be earning, because what you are really trying to gain is the positive credit rating obtained by having the account and making timely purchases. Also, be sure to look carefully at the fees associated with the cards.

In the event that you no longer want the secured credit card, simply contact the servicing company to close the account, and the deposit will be returned to you.

A third way to build credit is to have your purchase guaranteed by a **cosigner**. Your cosigner will put his or her credit on the line and vouch for your character and ability to repay the debt in a timely manner. In the event that you default on your payments, the debt becomes your cosigner's obligation. Too many people have had their credit destroyed by cosigning for a friend, family member, or business associate.

Obtaining credit for the first time can be difficult and frustrating. You need credit to get credit, but cannot get credit unless you have credit. While having a cosigner speed you along in the process is one of your options for obtaining credit, it is definitely not one that many people would choose.

Most people will be hesitant to cosign for someone, so rather than put friends and family in that awkward position, you may be better off accepting a higher interest rate and living with the payment for a year, and then refinancing once the twelve months have passed.

One final word of warning: while credit is necessary for most of us to purchase cars, homes, and college educations, it should not be used as a bridge to your next paycheck. Use credit responsibly, and know that once you ruin your credit, it will take at least seven years to repair it.

Guard your new credit and keep a vigilant eye on your credit reports. Actively correct mistakes and be wary of online purchases that look like they are insecure.

7

Paying Down Debt vs. Building Up Savings

I have often heard the question, should I pay down my debts or build up my savings? The answer is often long and drawn out, if not confusing. After all, the question is usually posed to a financial expert on a radio station or submitted via email, and each expert has a different view based on his or her own experience. Experts usually begin their answer with "it depends" and then start their oratory. At the end of their answer, the inquisitor is still left wondering what they should do.

My answer to the question of whether to pay down debts or build up savings is always "yes." Let me explain. I will address the question by covering each scenario independently.

First, consider the scenario in which you pay down your debts while committing no funds to savings. Where would you go to get money in the event that you did have an emergency? Unfortunately, you can't go to your savings because you don't have any. Also, while you have been doing a great job paying down your debts and making major strides, you now face the reality that others have faced before—you must now use the very cards that you have been paying off to cover your financial hurdle. Furthermore, you may find that while your efforts are commendable, each time you get close to paying off one card, something inevitably comes up, forcing you to turn to credit again and again. You have been placed on the hamster wheel. Only a long period with no changes in your financial life will allow you enough time to get off and move on to the next stage in your financial development.

In the other scenario, you choose to save in small savings accounts or even money market accounts while paying the monthly minimum on your credit cards and loans. Your savings are growing, earning anywhere between 0%–6%. You are feeling quite good because you are finally seeing growth in your savings, and now you can purchase what you want without pulling out a credit card. After inspecting your credit card statements, you notice that your credit card balances are not shrinking; in fact, some of them are going up month after month. This is where a lot of the financial gurus will say that you made your mistake. You have a savings account that is growing at about 6% a year, while your debts are growing at 20% or more. Reality is that you are still losing money as long as you are earning less on your savings than you are paying on your debts. Here is where my answer comes in as a resounding "yes" to the question of whether to save or pay down debts.

You earned your financial position one day at a time and will have to improve your position one day at a time. You did not end up mortgaged to the farthest reach of your earnings potential overnight. No, you got to where you are by making choices. To get out of debt and improve your financial position, you must make better choices.

You must pay down your debts because you are paying high interest rates and penalties and are subject to the wills of your creditors. You must also build up your savings so that you can minimize your reliance on creditors, friends, family members, and banks. Only by both saving and paying down your debts will you see both your savings grow and your debts decrease. Then, if you broke a tooth in the middle of the night, you would at least have savings to turn to.

By paying down your credit while increasing your savings, you will come to no longer rely on plastic and will be able to position yourself on the right track, one that leads to financial independence. So the next time you hear someone ask the question, should I pay down my debts or increase my savings? answer "yes" and explain why.

Unit 3: Money Matters

Plan for the Unexpected

I am often surprised when I see how shocked people are that they must pay for bills they knew were coming due. It takes just a small effort in a relatively short time to limit your financial surprises and thus improve your financial standing.

There are certain expenses that you have either annually or biennially that you know will be coming. Purchasing tires for your car is one of these; just because you don't know the frequency of the purchase doesn't keep the tires from wearing down every time you take a drive. Many people neglect to save up for this huge expense.

Every time you go to a repair shop, the mechanics let you know what the wear is on your tires. And yet, most people refuse to put the money away.

If you know that you are getting paid next Friday, don't you plan out how you will spend your money? Of course; you've laid out the bills and expenses that you have and the savings you will put away. You do this even though you know that the payday is more than a week away. Why not do the same for tires and other major expenses?

When you purchased your vehicle either new or used, chances are you paid attention to the tires. After you drove off the car lot, however, you no longer paid attention to the tires, even though they were the one item on the car that you could plan on having to replace soon.

While there are many types of tires, you should be familiar with the ones on your vehicle. Price them at tire shops, dealerships, and even online to discover how much this predictable expense will set you back, and begin saving. If they are 60-month or 60,000-mile tires, break the savings down into 60 months and place the money somewhere safe. This way, the next time you have to pay $1600 for a new set of tires, you don't need to skip a mortgage payment or refuse to take your child to the dentist for braces.

Planning ahead is one of the easiest steps you can take to limiting financial surprises. What other expenses do you know of that typically cost you a lot of money but you never seem to plan for? What about Thanksgiving and Christmas?

Many of us spend the most on our children and families during the Thanksgiving and Christmas holidays. While some people focus on travel and others on gift giving, surprisingly few seem to focus on planning. We are often surprised at how high the cost is when we postpone purchasing airline tickets for a family of five until November. We then make up excuses as to why we can't visit family this year even though we were looking forward to the trip. Then we have to call our families with another sob story about why we can't make the trip.

Why don't we purchase those tickets during the summer or early fall when the airlines put those particular tickets on sale?

Recently on CNN, there was a story covering one of the major airlines and their predictive pricing for flights. Their computer software incorporates the corporate budget outlining the required profit for the flight and prices tickets accordingly. It was alarming to see the disparity between ticket prices on the same flight. Furthermore, some seats were purposely left unsold as the airline waited for last-minute shoppers to pay top dollar to take those flights.

The software controls the profit margin, but you control how much your seat costs by purchasing your seat in advance. One particular passenger did not purchase only two weeks before; instead, he had purchased his seat over six months in advance and was grinning as he spoke of how inexpensive his seat was, especially when his price was compared to that of the person seated next to him.

Plan for the Unexpected

Most of us begin planning our next trip, vacation, or travel arrangements when we are just returning from another destination. Why then do we wait until the last minute to make arrangements for our next trip?

While you cannot predict what you will be doing one year from now, you can opt to purchase tickets that have refund options just in case your plans change. Additionally, buying these tickets early can save you a lot of money.

Holiday shopping can be brutal; we shop too much, we spend too much, and we spend all our money trying to make someone else happy and then spend the better part of three months miserable, trying to pay off the gifts we bought to make someone else feel good.

The holidays should not be about gifts, but about family and companionship. Your affection for loved ones should not be measured by how much you spend or how big the gift you purchased for them is.

Unfortunately, because we are constantly trying to outdo ourselves by purchasing a better gift this year than last year, many of us will overextend ourselves by blowing our holiday budgets. We spend too much and we start saving too late for what we want to buy. Now, because we got caught up in the spirit of the season, some bills will get paid in January that should have been paid in December.

This is step one on the fast track to financial turmoil. Unless you can get back on track, your new year will be off to a bad start.

If you plan your holiday budget in January, you can save all year and still bring joy to someone else while having financial peace of mind for yourself.

Did you know that most banks still offer holiday savings accounts? Most are easy to set up and use. Contact your bank to get the account set up, tell them how much money you want put away every month or paycheck, and the bank takes care of the rest. The bank will transfer the money out of your appointed account according to the schedule that you have set up. When it is time for you to shop, your account will already be funded. You can now spend, guilt free, up until the money runs out; you will feel good about yourself because you provided the gifts that you wanted rather than the ones you could afford. Your New Year's Day will not be filled with toil and trouble as you await the bills from the Christmas elves—Discover, Visa, and MasterCard.

To summarize, recognize that you cannot plan for every expense, but if you can somehow plan for the expenses you know that you will encounter in the short term, you will ensure that you stay on track for reaching your long-term goals.

Notice that I did not say that you should not travel or that you should not buy gifts. Also notice that I did not say you should not purchase what you would like to have. Instead, I implore you to plan these expenses early and save while you don't have to worry about them. As a result, you will put more money in your pockets.

So the next time a coworker is standing in the break room, complaining of an expensive tuition bill, tire change, or airline ticket, just smile and leave the room, because such negative banter is not for your ears—you no longer have that problem. Should you feel compelled to discuss anything with him or her, suggest that he or she reads this chapter or buy this book and then come back to discuss his or her findings with you.

We don't plan to fail, but we unfortunately fail to plan, and not having a plan can lead to major problems when it comes to managing your finances. To make a difference in your financial future, begin planning today for the expected so that you will minimize your unexpected expenses.

To get an idea of which expenses to plan for, gather up your bank and credit card statements and look for all the major purchases, defined as any expense greater than $500 or the amount you currently have in your savings and checking account. These expenses, while surprises in the past, should never come back up because you are preparing yourself for them both mentally and financially.

Plan for the Unexpected

Though you may still gripe about having to make the purchase, I am sure that afterward you will smile as you tell your friends, family, and coworkers that you had to pay $1200 for new tires.

Net Worth

Before we discuss your financials and begin to make changes to your financial status, we first must develop a starting point—your net worth, the one number that all financial professionals will recognize.

In geography, you learned about maps. Planning a trip using a map requires two distinct positions. The first position is where you are or where you will be starting from. The latter position, necessary to plan a trip on a map, is the point that you are trying to arrive at or are going to. If you don't have either of these points then you can end up anywhere. Unfortunately, anywhere is not where you were hoping to go. We always have a destination in mind, but all too often we skip this part of the planning phase and just start our journey, hoping to arrive where we would like to be.

If I blindfolded you, dropped you off in a foreign city, and told you to find your way home, chances are you would have trouble doing so as long as you did not know where you were.

If instead I dropped you off with a map, told you where you were, and then told you to find your way home, you could do so because you would then have a starting position. Your starting position in personal finances is your net worth.

Your net worth tells bankers, creditors, and the world how much you are worth.

Mathematically, your **net worth** is equal to your assets minus your liabilities.

Put in other words, your net worth is equal to what you own after you subtract what you owe. This number is far more important than your salary or personal income, though typically when people speak of their net worth, they refer to their income. The inherent flaw in counting on your income is that you could be laid off tomorrow. Then what would you have? A large mortgage, an auto lease or two, and a lot of credit card bills.

Your net worth is more important than your income. To increase your net worth, do two things: first, increase assets, and second, decrease liabilities.

Another term that is important for you to know is your **liquid net worth**. Your liquid net worth includes only those assets that can be liquidated in a very short period of time. These assets include cash, mutual funds, stocks, options, certificates of deposits, savings bonds, and other investments. Your home, cars, jewelry, limited partnerships, real estate, and possessions are not included, as these assets typically take a longer time to liquidate and usually go at "fire sale" rates.

Net Worth = Assets – Liabilities
To increase net worth:
↑ Assets
↓ Liabilities

You should have some idea of what your net worth is. Your goal is to increase it annually. Corporations compute and report their net worth quarterly to bondholders (creditors) and shareholders (investors). Those companies with an increasing net worth are rewarded with more investors, while those with a decreasing net worth are penalized by both investors and creditors.

Similarly, you too should compute your net worth annually because you too are judged by this number. Knowing your current financial position is the first step on your way to financial success. Using the table on the next page, compute your current net worth:

How much are you worth?
(Use Table 3 below to compute.)

Net Worth   =   Assets – Liabilities

_____   =   _____ – _____

Great! You now know your current financial position. Your number may be negative, which is perfectly okay, since where you start does not have to be where you finish. All a negative number means is that you have some catching up to do before you reach your financial goals. If your net worth is a positive number, then you have a bit of a head start, but you can still improve your financial position.

Remember, it is very important to know where you are starting.

The remainder of these exercises will help you to figure out where you are going and how you will get there.

ASSETS	AMOUNT	LIABILITIES	AMOUNT
Checking	$	Credit Card 1	$
Savings	$	Credit Card 2	$
Money Markets	$	Credit Card 3	$
CDs	$	Credit Card 4	$
US Savings Bond 1	$	Credit Card 5	$
US Savings Bond 2	$	Credit Card 6	$
401(k)	$	Credit Card 7	$
403(b)	$	Credit Card 8	$
Traditional IRA	$	Credit Card 9	$
Roth IRA	$	Credit Card 10	$
Education IRA	$	Mortgage	$
SEP IRA	$	Second Mortgage	$
SIMPLE IRA	$	Auto Loan 1	$
Mutual Funds	$	Auto Loan 2	$
Stocks	$	Student Loan 1	$
Bonds	$	Student Loans 2	$
Real Estate	$	Other Loans	$
Total Assets	**$**	**Total Liabilities**	**$**

Table 3: Net Worth Calculation

At this point, I am going to ask you to make a commitment that your current net worth, whether positive or negative, will be the worst financial position that you will be in for the remainder of your life. Strive to improve that number and do everything in your power to protect your financial position. Put simply, you should be looking up from here, and the number that you wrote today should be your floor. This commitment will become the cornerstone for everything that you do as you improve your financial position.

This next section will describe your journey as you improve your financial position. No longer should you be content with just paying bills and saving money; you should now begin to create wealth.

Three Phases of Wealth

Over the span of your adult life, you will go through three phases of wealth. These phases are wealth accumulation, wealth distribution, and wealth transfer. Barring an early death, most of us will go through these phases.

Wealth Accumulation

This phase begins at the age of majority and ends at retirement, at whatever that age may be. In other words, this phase starts when you turn eighteen and start working, and ends when you stop working due to retirement. This is the savings and investments period. Employer-sponsored retirement plans, IRAs, stocks, bonds, mutual funds, and real estate are common in this phase.

Wealth Distribution

When you decide to retire, you will live off of what you have accumulated. The better the job you did during the accumulation phase, the better your lifestyle will be during retirement.

Social Security and Medicare may play a part for those who are eligible. Some people find that their accumulations are not enough to support them for the length of their retirement. As a result, some return to work, others move in with family, and others must depend on the government and their communities for support.

Wealth Transfer

The old adage saying that the only two things sure in life are death and taxes applies in part to this phase of wealth. During this phase, your remaining assets are distributed to heirs and beneficiaries, and your final expenses are covered. Wills and trusts play a big role in this phase. The more prepared you are when this phase comes around, the more assets your beneficiaries and heirs will receive.

10

Monthly Spending Estimate

Now that you know what your net worth is and you have committed to making improvements to your financial position, focus on your income and outgoing expenses.

Your income is fixed as long as you are at your current place of employment. You may make minor changes to it, but for the most part, your income won't be changing much. Unfortunately, this is out of your control. You can, however, work on your outgoing expenses, because you control what you spend your money on.

The approach you will take to create your spending plan will be to first, estimate your monthly spending, next, track your spending, and last, create a spending plan.

A **spending plan** is a detailed document that you create to manage your outgoing income. Unlike a budget, in which you are constantly reminded to give up certain expenses, a spending plan takes a more positive approach to helping you manage your money. You include everything that you would like to spend money on and the desired amount, and, if necessary, make adjustments to cover any shortfalls. Once completed, you have a monthly roadmap you can follow that puts you in total control of your finances.

Being less restrictive and more inclusive of nonessential items ensures that you will stick to the plan. You go through so much effort in the beginning so that you can first find the leaky pipe in the house rather, than ripping out all of the plumbing and just starting over. To fix the problems that you are having with overspending, you must find out where you are weakest and begin to change that behavior.

Most people don't recognize that they have a spending problem or that they earn more than they really do simply because they get so accustomed to just spending whatever the payroll department deposits into their accounts. Recognize your spending problems, like a child who looks down to notice that he is bleeding. Before he takes that first look, he couldn't feel any pain and didn't know that he was hurting, but after that first glance he recognizes that he is injured and the pain begins to reverberate throughout his body.

In much the same way, we bleed away money unknowingly, without regard to how we are hurting ourselves in the long term. By completing the exercises in this chapter, your eyes will open and you will recognize areas in which you can improve.

You must first figure out what you are currently spending your money on. To accomplish this task you will need to gather some of your financial records. Use your checkbook register, credit card statements, bank statements, and any financial software that you have to find the information necessary to complete the worksheets on the following pages.

The Monthly Expense Worksheet (Table 4) includes a number of monthly expenses that you would likely spend money on. The purpose of the worksheet is to account for all money going out of your household and to expose any surplus or shortages in monthly income that are not accounted for, as any funds in excess of your planned expenses typically get lost.

Have you ever received your paycheck, paid all of your bills, and thought that you would have $400 left over to put away in savings, only to discover that nothing was available a week later? Moreover, have you ever wondered where that extra money went? Do you believe you should have an extra $200 per paycheck free for savings but cannot seem to find it once all of your expenses are paid for?

These missing funds are not being stolen by the sock gremlin, but instead are slipping through the cracks on unplanned or unnecessary expenses. Maybe they satisfied some surprise expense, but more often the excess funds went toward something that you cannot recall or are no longer enjoying.

Stop and take a moment to fill in Table 4 using the information that you have gathered. Estimate any value that you cannot readily find. As you continue in the process, you will be able to be more precise. Write the information directly in the book—it's okay, you paid for it! Have your friends buy their own copies.

Knowing what your expenses are on a monthly basis can be essential in the event that you become unemployed or face a financial emergency. You may also find these numbers useful when considering new employment opportunities. If you are earning enough to cover the expenses that you have, then you should be able to use the additional funds for your other financial goals.

Expense	Monthly Amount	Expense	Monthly Amount
Mortgage/Rent	$	Groceries/Supplies	$
Taxes/Insurance	$	Lawn Care	$
Auto Loans/Leases	$	Maid Service	$
Security	$	Pool Care	$
Water/Sewer/Garbage	$	Gasoline/Fuel	$
Telephone/Internet	$	Parking/Tolls	$
Cell Phone	$	Inspection/Registration	$
Gas	$	Auto Maintenance	$
Electric	$	Home Maintenance	$
Cable/Satellite	$	Haircuts/Tanning/Nails	$
Auto Insurance	$	Tobacco/Cigarettes	$
Life Insurance	$	Pet Food/Expenses	$
Health Insurance	$	Gifts	$
Credit Card Payments	$	Entertainment	$
Loans	$	Clothing	$
Child Support/ Alimony	$	Dry Cleaning	$
Educational Expenses	$	Dining out	$
Charitable Contributions	$	Medical	$
Savings	$	Other	$
Total (Column 1)	$	**Total (Column 2)**	$

Table 4: Monthly Expense Worksheet

You must also account for your income on a monthly basis in order to make the spending plan a success. In Table 5, please enter your net (take-home) income for a month.

Net Income By Source	Monthly Amount
Earner 1	$
Earner 2	$
Child Support/Alimony	$
Social Security	$
Retirement Plan/Pension	$
Rental Sources	$
Investment Income	$
Other	$
Total Net Income	$

Table 5: Monthly Income

Now that you know what's coming into and what's going out of your household, let's see if there is a surplus or a shortage of income. Enter the information from the previous tables into the equation below.

Net Surplus/Shortage = Total Net Income – Total (Column 1) – Total (Column 2)

_____ = _____ – _____ – _____

Looking at your net surplus/shortage, does the number you wrote down make sense to you? Are you surprised to it? If you are thinking that the number is incorrect and that something must be wrong, then you do have a slight problem.

If the number is negative, you are spending more than you are bringing home and have probably noticed that you have to pull out your credit cards a lot more than you used to. The evidence will be seen in the increasing balances of the cards and the decreasing balance of your savings accounts.

Furthermore, a negative number means that you have to make some adjustments to come back into balance. Remember, your income isn't going to change that much. There are some strategies you can use to increase your take-home pay, but overall, you have what you earn and you must do the best that you can to make it fit your lifestyle. The next step will help you to identify areas where you may be spending more than you think and will also help to highlight areas where you can make some changes.

On the other hand, if the number is positive, you are earning more than you are spending, which is good. If the number is more than you are accustomed to having left over at the end of the month, then you have discovered the problem; you have money that is mysteriously disappearing.

To truly be successful, you must account for every dollar coming in and going out. The balance sheet must be accurate. If funds are not accounted for, they will get lost in the day-to-day operation of your life. Money earned that has no place to go will find some place to go, but you won't benefit from it. So, if you have a surplus as noted in the equation above, then apply the additional funds to some of your other financial goals.

11

Track Your Expenses

The next step in getting your finances in order is tracking your expenses. We have looked at what you have typically spent on bills and other household expenses as evidenced by your financial software, checkbook, and financial statements. We will now turn our attention to the spending that you may not recognize you are doing. To do so you will need to purchase a 2" x 4" steno pad and carry it with you during the next two weeks. During these next two weeks, your task is to record everything that you spend. It will only take you a moment to record the purchases that you make, but it will dramatically increase the accuracy of your spending plan.

The goal at this point is not to change any of your spending habits. If you would like a soda and feel like purchasing one at the vending machine in your break room, then go ahead—just make sure to jot down the purchase when you get back to your desk. At first, this task may seem a bit overwhelming and you will most certainly find yourself wanting to quit or to skip this step, but in the end the hard work will pay off if you can stick with it. Remember that financial independence is not an easy thing to accomplish and that most people do not attain it, mainly because they are unwilling to make certain changes. If success was easy, then everyone would achieve it. Also, remember that successful people always do what unsuccessful people are unwilling to do. I implore you to stick with this program for the next two weeks.

Day by day you must remember to grab the pad and place it in your purse or pocket. Place a pen next to the pad when you go to sleep at night and place both items next to your keys so that you will remember to bring them along when you leave in the morning. If you spend any money, any at all, write the purchase on the pad. The entry can simply be "Sprite $1.29" or "Gas $35.00." You don't need to record taxes or where you purchase the items, just the item that you purchased and the amount you paid.

Here are a few simple guidelines that will help you to accomplish the task:

1. Keep receipts from purchases so that you can separate the items at a convenient time.
2. Purchases such as groceries or dry cleaning should not be itemized but listed as a category.
3. Items that fall under different categories on the same receipt should be recorded in their respective categories, e.g., snacks, fuel, oil change, etc.
4. Vending machine items should always be listed, and the same goes for impulse purchases.
5. Bill payments should be listed under their category name, e.g., electric, gas, cell phone, etc.
6. Do not try to analyze the purchases. Just jot down the entry and put the pad away until your next purchase.
7. Don't forget items that you may not notice on a daily basis, such as tolls for turnpikes or travel.
8. If there are multiple people in your household, give each one a pad to record his or her purchases.
9. Be honest.

At the end of the two weeks you should have a fairly good representation of what you spend your money on every month. Some people will be shocked to discover that $30–$50 a month is spent at the vending machines in their offices. Others may notice that they spend over $200 per month at Starbucks or the local coffee shop. The first time I did this exercise, I noticed that

Track Your Expenses

I was spending $60 per month at one fast food restaurant for breakfast and over $100 per month a few hours later when I came back for lunch. My snack purchases were even worse. My job required me to drive around all day, so I spent most of my time going from my car to my clients' offices and then back to the car again. I wasted so much money during the first two years that I could never understand why I always had to turn to a credit card to cover expenses at the end of the month. My goal is that you too will make similar discoveries.

Your next step will be to total up all of the spending by category and record the amounts on a blank sheet of paper. Be sure to gather up every pad that you previously gave out so that you can accurately reflect the household's spending as one unit. Often, overspending results when each spouse is not aware of what the other is purchasing. Financial rifts form in families when one member consistently overspends while another is trying to save. This exercise is meant to bring everyone back to the table for a discussion of what is coming in and what is going out of the household in terms of money.

While your tracking exercise lasted for two weeks, your spending plan will use a model period of one month, so double the amounts that you have so that the totals represent four weeks, or approximately one month.

Compare what you originally recorded on your expenses worksheet in the previous chapter to the amounts that you have recorded for each category after tracking your spending. Do you notice any trends? Are there any surprises? If the number that you originally used on the expense worksheet is less than what you are actually spending, use the greater number for your spending plan. If the amount is less than your originally expected amount, keep the estimated or expected number, since some categories will vary slightly from month to month and you don't want you to come up over budget.

Tracking your spending also allows you to identify places where you may not be maximizing your spending dollar. For instance, if you notice that you are purchasing two Cokes a day at work for $1 each, you may benefit from purchasing a case of Coke at your local store for $8–$10 and saving yourself $10 per week. You will be getting the same satisfaction of drinking your two Cokes, but at half the price. The same applies to your snack purchases. Identifying ways you can make improvements in your spending is paramount to the success of any budget planning process.

In the next chapter, we will put everything together and demonstrate how to accurately use the spending plan to control your household's spending. The plans will become a utility that you can use, reference, and make adjustments to throughout the year. In business terms, you are being promoted to Chief Financial Officer (CFO) of your household. You must report your findings to your family at monthly financial meetings and govern your family's spending according the plan that you all developed together.

12

My Spending Plan

Hopefully you are getting the hang of identifying areas of your spending where you may be able to make some changes. Typically our overages or conveniences are where we notice that we can make some improvements in our lives. Now we will begin to put together your spending plan, which will act as the foundation for your household operations. Later, we will discuss specific goals that you would like to accomplish.

Table 6 will be used to create your spending plan. Notice that it is similar to the expenses worksheet, but with the addition of new columns, one for budgeted or planned amounts and an additional column for actual amounts spent. As you go through the exercise, the use of the plan will become clearer.

Before you begin, identify the number of pay periods you have each year. Do you receive your paychecks weekly (52), every two weeks (26), on the 1st and 15th or 15th and 30th (24), or monthly (12)? The number of pay periods you have will be used to determine how often you will update your spending plan and thus determine how many copies of the worksheet you should create. If you have access to computer software that will allow you to create the worksheet in a spreadsheet, then by all means, do so. The main idea is that you must complete the exercises in order to see the positive effects that planning can make in your financial life.

Expense	Planned	Actual	Over/Under
Mortgage/Rent	$	$	
Taxes/Insurance	$	$	
Auto Loan/Lease	$	$	
Security	$	$	
Water/Sewer/Garbage	$	$	
Telephone/Internet	$	$	
Cell Phone	$	$	
Gas	$	$	
Electric	$	$	
Cable/Satellite	$	$	
Auto Insurance	$	$	
Life Insurance	$	$	
Health Insurance	$	$	
Credit Cards	$	$	
Loans	$	$	
Child Support/Alimony	$	$	
Educational Expenses	$	$	
Charitable Contributions	$	$	
Savings	$	$	
Groceries/Household	$	$	
Lawn Care	$	$	
Maid Service	$	$	
Pool Care	$	$	
Gasoline/Fuel	$	$	
Parking/Tolls	$	$	
Inspection/Registration	$	$	
Auto Maintenance	$	$	
Home Maintenance	$	$	
Haircuts/Tanning/Nails	$	$	
Tobacco/Cigarettes	$	$	
Pet Food/Expenses	$	$	
Gifts	$	$	
Entertainment	$	$	
Clothing	$	$	
Dry Cleaning	$	$	
Dining Out	$	$	
Medical	$	$	
Other	$	$	

Table 6: Spending Plan

My Spending Plan

The reason that the number of pay periods is important is that you will be filling out the spending worksheets in the same way that you make purchases. You probably make purchases during the weeks that you receive your compensation. You likely purchase food, increase your eating out, resume shopping, and pay bills almost immediately after your pay is received. The numbers that you recorded in the expense worksheet that you later updated after the tracking exercise will be used to create the planned amounts for each category in the spending plan worksheet. The major difference will be that you will have to split up some of the expenses to reflect your normal purchasing habits.

For example, you pay your rent or mortgage once a month, so this expense will not be split. If, however, you are paid weekly, you may purchase groceries once a week instead of once a month. This weekly purchase of groceries lets you know that you should enter a weekly value for food purchases in the spending plan, rather than the monthly number that you came up with previously. A planned grocery amount of $400 can be split into $100 per week in this case.

Let's continue with our example of $100 per week spent on groceries. If, in one week, you purchase $125 in groceries because of some good sales, then in the worksheet you would reflect the actual amount spent as well as the overage. To stay on budget and not lose control of your plan, you must now make an adjustment because of the $25 overage. The quickest way to do so is to decrease the planned amount for the next week. Next week's planned grocery spending amount will now be $75 instead of $100. If you are able to stay within your budgeted amount during this week, then the following week (week three in this case) would return to the originally planned amount of $100.

Conversely, if instead of spending $125 on groceries, you only spent $80, then since you are under budget, you have a choice. You may choose to increase the spending level for the following week, or you may move that additional $20 into a savings account. If you choose to increase the grocery limit, then you have increased shopping flexibility for the next week.

If the trend continues and you are consistently under budget, then you can make the adjustment to your planned amount and continue to build up your savings. This decision is totally up to you. You may decide that any extra money gets allocated to a specific account where money goes in but only comes out for emergencies, or you may choose to spend the money on something that is not in the plan. If you do the latter, it will take a longer time for you to experience the effects that having a plan provides. As long as you go around the plan, you are not truly following the system and you'll always find an excuse when you want to justify making an impulse purchase.

To recap, for each period you will have an assigned amount for each category that you recorded in your plan. If you go over budget then you must bring yourself back in to compliance by penalizing yourself during the next period. If you are under budget, then you reward yourself by having a temporary increased limit or by allowing yourself to apply the funds to a different category, such as savings. This process will continue pay period after pay period. After three months, the process will become automatic and you won't give the plan a second thought; you may even wonder how you ever got along without it. More importantly, you will begin to notice some increases in your savings account, along with the progress that you are making in repaying your credit card debt.

Remember that you should not have many surprises because you accounted for everything in your expense worksheet. You may experience some times where the amount that you budgeted was not enough for a repair or for another unexpected expense, but everything should be planned out, which brings us to the next area of discussion.

What happens when the expenses that you have budgeted for do not occur, such as auto repairs or household repairs? Remember that you are saving for certain expenses in advance because you know that they will come due in the future. A vacation is easier to pay for if you save up for it monthly. Tires are easier to purchase if you are prepaying for them instead of having to come up with a lump sum in a moment's notice. In essence, what you are doing is setting aside money for these expenses that you know are going to happen. These funds should be set aside in an account and the breakdown of each category should be logged, so that you know how much of the available funds in the account are allocated to a particular category. When you spend in that particular category, update your records. If you overspend and therefore have to use funds from a different category, reflect the negative balance in your records and make up the deficit as you make deposits. As successful people say, create your plan, then work your plan.

As CFO of your household, your ability to stay on budget will determine how successful you can be. In time, you will notice that your financial situation is improving, your debts are diminishing, and your happiness is reaching new heights. As opportunities arise, you will be more prepared to consider them, instead of wishing that you were in a position to even dream of them.

One of the biggest problems that I see is that most people do not know how much money they really need for their household to survive. Most of us create lifestyles to accommodate our incomes. We make big purchases, pay top dollar, and must have the newest items. Our vehicles become more expensive and we sign up for any service that will make our lives easier. We don't make these purchases out of necessity; we simply choose to do so because we can afford it. Unfortunately, what we should be thinking to ourselves is, do I need this right now?

I have heard it said that most Americans are just one paycheck away from being on the street. In a recession where 40% of a person's retirement account could disappear overnight, I am ready to believe. Our current economic system is fragile at best. Economists are saying that we came out of the most recent recession early in 2009 and that the economy will be stabilizing if consumers will keep spending. The sad truth is that most of us just cannot afford to keep the economy afloat. Many Americans who previously could afford their lifestyles are out of work due to layoffs. Suddenly, there is no income and no prospect for work, leaving able-bodied wage earners on the sidelines, wishing for improvements.

Please don't take this the wrong way, but in 2008 and 2009, unemployment benefits were extended well past ordinary limits. At the time of this writing, the documents that must be signed to keep extended benefits coming in 2010 are sitting in Congress awaiting approval. Without them, many people's unemployment benefits will begin to dry up.

For some people, unemployment benefits are sufficient to maintain a household. Unfortunately, for many high wage earners this is not the case. If used correctly, though, the unemployment benefits can cover most of the necessary expenses of the average household of four. In the case where benefits may not be able meet all of their households' needs, wage earners are finding ways to cut back on monthly expenses to bridge the gap.

Having your expenses written down and easily accessible will enable you to make hard decisions in the event that you are affected by the next economic downturn or if your income is abruptly stopped. In times of crisis, you will see where your priorities lie. All of a sudden, you don't need cable, and season tickets to the local sports team are not that important. Used cars become as good as new cars, and so on. Things that you swore you would never eat, places you would never shop, even clothes that you would never wear start to look a bit more appealing.

The problem that most Americans face is that they don't know where their money goes; they have an idea, but not an accurate accounting of what they spend money on. Just like on a map, if you don't know where you are currently, how can you expect to get to where you want to go? So how can you make changes to your finances if you don't know everything that you spend money on right now? By doing the exercises in this chapter, you have stopped to assess your situation before trying to determine possible solutions.

13

Taxes

Before you begin this section, please note that I am not a tax adviser, nor do I intend for this section to offer any advice on taxes. Please consult with your tax adviser before making any changes or adjustments to any of your tax forms. I would, however, like to make sure that you are aware of a few pieces of information that are critical to you and your family's finances.

The United States internal revenue tax code is long and complicated. Year after year, thousands of changes are put into the tax code, and more often than not, the Internal Revenue Service (IRS) will offer guidance to make sure that everyone is in compliance. As a wage earner in this country, it is not easily possible for you to work a full-time job and then familiarize yourself with all of the tax laws that might benefit you. Professionals, such as enrolled agents, certified public accountants, and other tax advisers spend the majority of their days wrestling with and navigating through the complex web of tax laws and guidelines, so they are better suited to handle your tax questions. If you are committed to the do-it-yourself approach, you can contact the IRS yourself to have your questions answered. For the purposes of this text, my recommendation is that you seek a professional tax adviser to help you with even the simplest of tax filings or tax questions.

Income taxes paid by tax payers are determined by two methods, an **alternative minimum tax calculation** and a **graduated system.**

The alternative minimum tax (AMT) acts as a parallel system to the graduated tax system that most Americans are accustomed to. Your tax professional will compute your taxes using both methods to determine whether or not you should be filing under the alternative minimum tax. Unfortunately, the AMT is well outside the scope of this text. The AMT was designed to ensure that every taxpayer had to pay at least some taxes. Wage earners in the higher income tax brackets may find themselves filing their income taxes using the AMT calculation.

The graduated system is what most people refer to when they mention their tax bracket. The tax bracket that they are referring to is the percentage of taxes that they are required to pay based on the income they earn. Most people believe that there is only one tax rate; there are actually, however, two.

The first and the most common is the **marginal tax rate**. The marginal tax rate is the percentage of taxes the taxpayer would pay if they were to earn one more dollar at the end of the year. Just like margins on a paper, your marginal tax bracket has a lower limit and an upper limit. Most everyone can identify their marginal tax rate as one of the numbers below:

10%	15%	25%	28%	33%	35%

Many people are not aware that there is an **effective tax rate**, which is the percentage of taxes the taxpayer actually pays after all deductions and exemptions are claimed. The effective tax rate is the summation of each of the tax liabilities from the lower tax brackets added to the percentage of income earned in the current tax bracket. When you divide the amount of taxes you actually paid by the amount that you earned, you will notice that the percentage is lower than the marginal rate that you identified yourself as having. This difference in the two rates is the main reason that most people have larger tax refunds or smaller tax-due bills at filing time.

Many people can control their take home-pay with greater certainty if they know what their effective tax rate is. When you sign your tax filing document, you are agreeing that the amount you are entering is the amount of your overpayment or underpayment, and that you are therefore either due a refund or must pay the shortfall. The reason the overpayment or underpayment exists is that the amount of your withholdings is an estimate that you set up at the beginning of the year or when you sign on with a new employer mid-year. The amount of your withholdings is determined when you fill out Form W-4.

On this form, you declare the number of allowances for the employer to use when calculating the withholding amount from your check for prepayment of your income taxes. This withholding amount appears as a line item on your check stub. Form W-4 has two worksheets on it to help you determine the correct number of allowances. It even has a place for you to detach the worksheets from the section of the form that is required, although most people do not detach the top of the form. If you look closely at Form W-4, you will see a line that asks if you would like to add an additional withholding amount in anticipation of your tax bill at the end of the year.

These sections are often overlooked, and most people are not truly aware of how to fill out the form. In fact, some people still fill out Form W-4 in the same manner that they did when they got their first job. They select "single" with zero allowances and then sign the form and turn it in. They do not know why—they just know that their parents told them to do so when they were young, and no one has ever explained anything different to them.

Contrary to popular belief, exemptions are different than allowances. **Exemptions** reduce the amount of income that is subject to the graduated system.

When you file your taxes, you claim the exemptions that you are eligible for, along with the deductions that you qualify for, in order to determine the taxes that you should have paid. This amount is then compared to the amount that you have already paid to determine either your refund or your taxes-due bill.

Properly filling out Form W-4 can help you more closely approximate your payroll deductions, which could lead to improvements in your take-home pay each pay period. You must keep in mind that any adjustments made will affect your tax refund or tax-due status. Before you make any changes, consult your tax professional. Have him or her explain the form to you until you understand what you are filling out, and then get his or her guidance on filling out the form according to your financial situation.

Many people believe that having a large tax return is the way to go; often, you will hear of them bragging about how large their return was, as though it were a contest. The IRS wants each taxpayer to pay his or her fair share and no more than that. This is the why you as a taxpayer receive income tax refunds or must make up for deficits when filing your taxes.

Having a large tax refund is a mistake. Experts acknowledge that you are not earning any interest on funds that are overpaid in taxes and returned in the form of a tax refund. Furthermore, most of the recipients of large tax refunds could benefit from having the extra income in their households throughout the year.

When was the last time you went into a bank and requested a loan? Did they tell you to just pay them back next year, or did you have a conversation about interest rates? Did you have to shop around with different banks to get a rate that you like? Could you request a zero-interest loan from the bank, and not be escorted out the door?

Would you lend money to a bank and not expect any interest in return? You, as a wage earner, work very hard for your money, trading your time for it. When you give away your money without earning interest, then in reality you are actually wasting your time. Your money should always work as hard for you as you work to obtain it.

Giving away your money interest-free is like paying your friend's utility bills with your utility bill money. You sit around and hope that he or she will give the money back soon so that you can pay your bills. Unfortunately, he or she pays you back on his or her own schedule, which leaves you sitting in the dark. How are those candles working for you? You are sitting around hoping and praying that your friend drops by with your repayment. Interest-free loans make just as much sense.

Taxes

Just as there's no such thing as a free lunch, everything has a cost. You pay for lending money without payment in opportunity cost—you miss out on opportunities while your money is not in your possession.

Is the IRS doing anything wrong? No, they are not even doing you a disservice; *you* are making the mistake by not taking advantage of the tax laws and filing opportunities that you are entitled to. You must ensure that the proper withholdings are deducted from your paycheck.

When filled out properly, Form W-4, which can be obtained from your employer or at *www.irs.gov*, can be used to closely approximate your end-of-year tax-due amount and can minimize the amount of your tax refund or tax-due bill. Before you run out and get another form and start making changes, I suggest that you gather your last three tax returns, a copy of your current Form W-4, and a blank copy of Form W-4, and make an appointment with your tax adviser. Have the tax adviser conduct a tax review and help you fill out the form in the proper manner, based off your past returns and your current financial position.

Inform the tax adviser that you would like to maximize your earning potential while limiting your tax refund.

Typically your tax advisor will be able to limit your tax refund or liability to $500 a year, which is good. With the additional funds, build up your savings or work toward your repayment plans. Wherever you place the funds, make them work for you. Remember you will no longer be receiving the large tax refunds that you are accustomed to. Now is not the time to begin having parties and going on shopping sprees; stay disciplined and remember the long-term goals you have for yourself.

I have heard many people say that the only way they can force themselves to save is by putting away their tax refund checks year after year. They rely on this as a savings vehicle because they are not disciplined enough to not spend the money if the funds were placed into their bank account each pay period.

If you are one of those people, then keep doing exactly what you are doing. Sticking to a spending and savings plan requires commitment and discipline, and if you have tried and failed many times before and the only success you have is by putting away your tax refund, then at least you have a system.

One last note about Form W-4 is that you are not limited to filling out only one of these forms per year. If your financial situation changes and you deem it necessary to make a change to your form, contact your payroll department to fill out a new one, keeping in mind that each employer has their own rules as to how often you can update the form. The responsibility in keeping the information up to date is yours!

Use this introduction to gain more information about the factors we have discussed and how they affect your net income.

Unit 4: Understanding Financial Matters

14

Financial Literacy

When was the last time you sat and spoke with your family about financial news? Have you ever discussed portfolios, asset allocation, or dollar cost averaging? Do you know what the Dow Jones Industrial Average, the Standard and Poor's 500, or the NASDAQ are? If asked, could you identify the current chairperson of the Federal Reserve, affectionately referred to as the Fed? Does the mere mention of these terms make you want to leave the room?

Quickly, can you recall which teams played this week? Can you identify which celebrity just got married or divorced? Do you know which of your favorite artists has a new album or what happened during last night's shows on TV?

Chances are, you had a lot more affirmative answers for the latter than you did for the former set of questions. It is amazing how we can collect so much useless trivia but shy away from learning things that will help or will mean something to us in the future.

To become successful financially, you should develop a more mature mindset. Rather than thinking of gossip and TV shows, begin to think of finances more often. You will have a more positive view of financial terms, news, and products. Before you can make the changes necessary to impact your life on a permanent basis, some of your viewpoints must change. Many of your friends will not understand your newfound interests, but you will attract a new set of friends who will be more interested in financial advancement than American Idol. In a short time, your knowledge of financial markets, investments, and insurance products will increase. Your newfound interest will mean smarter ways for you to save and better ways for you to invest. All of a sudden, your 401(k) will begin to make sense. You will know and understand what products you are being offered every time you go inside your local bank. The term CD will no longer represent compact discs for your stereo.

I am not saying that I want you to become a financial expert. Instead, I want you to have a working knowledge of financial matters. When an offer is presented to you, you should have some understanding of what you are hearing and know immediately if you should just ignore the conversation and move on.

Since no one taught you about balancing checkbooks, investments, or how to save for goals in school, you need to teach yourself by reading financial publications, journals, and websites. You will quickly discover that some information has a slant toward advertising rather than education, so be careful to evaluate the source before you take on any new endeavors.

The time you invest in becoming familiar with financial matters will be exponentially returned to you by a lifetime of knowledge and curiosity. How much time you spend improving your financial literacy is up to you, but reading an article a day should spark sufficient curiosity in you. After twenty-eight days, you will form a habit that you can count on lasting a long time. As you read more and more, you will begin to compare your personal finances with what you have been reading about.

Start with the *Wall Street Journal* or read the business page of your local newspaper. Visit MSN.com's money page or go to the Yahoo or Google money pages and just start reading. Some headlines will spark your curiosity, while others will bore you. Don't try to guide your learning by selecting specific topics to read about. Instead, just read what grabs your attention; the article's writer will surely have placed enough financial jargon in the article to satisfy your goal of learning. Good writers will also have offered some contextual clues to go along with unfamiliar terms.

Once you have read the article, put it away. Make mental notes about what you have read as the day goes on. Before long, your financial IQ will soar and you will become a source of knowledge for your family. The more articles you read, the more questions you will begin to find answers to.

If you are reluctant to try reading because of a lack of interest, I challenge you to step outside of your comfort zone. Your comfort zone has probably included savings accounts, checking accounts, certificates of deposit, 401(k) plans, and individual retirement accounts. There are many other instruments that can help you reach virtually any financial goal if you are experienced, knowledgeable, and sophisticated enough to try them. I recommend that you have some exposure to these investments prior to listening to any financial presentation.

Often when we sit down with a sales representative we are at a disadvantage; he or she knows more than we do. We don't even know what we don't know, and we're therefore not prepared to ask specific questions relevant to our decision-making process. Unfortunately, this lack of knowledge can cause us to become frustrated to the point that we just leave. Our ignorance can cause us to miss out on some good opportunities.

On the other hand, we may become hypnotized by the salesperson and the sales presentation, resulting in our agreeing to participate in programs that do not fit our needs. Ashamed, some of us will not call back during the proper timeframe to rescind our decision.

I recommend that you read financial publications, at least one per day for ten to fifteen minutes to make sure that you are as prepared as a Boy Scout. Share what you have learned with someone you trust. Get his or her input on it and make a game of learning. At lunch, discuss finances instead of sports or gossip. Remember, a smart consumer is an informed consumer, and, as we tell our children, reading is fundamental.

15

Savings and Savings Accounts

I can still hear my mother telling me to take a portion of my check and put it away for a rainy day. "A man should never be completely broke and should always have an emergency fund," she would say with a stern yet supportive look. Being seventeen years old, I tried to listen but never really put the advice into practice. Looking back, I wish I would have taken her advice more seriously.

Instead, I did what most people did when I got a job that paid decent—I shopped! Not only did I shop for myself, but I also bought gifts for my loved ones. Sure, I opened an account and I put money in, but the urge to spend was just too great. In time, I had everything that I wanted, but I never made any progress in the savings department. Instead of building up my account, I loaded up my room with stuff. Today, I can't list more than five things I bought with that money, although I recall a lot of trips to Jack in the Box, McDonald's, and Mr. Gatti's Pizza. If I could go back and save just 10% of the money that I've earned since I started working, I could probably buy ocean-side properties in California.

Unfortunately, I had only one class during grade school that discussed anything financial. We were taught in this class to balance checkbooks and to write checks. There was no mention of asset building, wealth accumulation, or even simple basic savings principles. Instead of learning about money, something that would shape my life from that time forward, I learned a lot about the arts, literature, and even basic speech writing. Looking back,

I wish my educators had taught me how to handle money correctly, how to position myself without debts, and how to look for financial opportunities.

With my lack of knowledge, I moved on to college and fell into the credit card trap. I traded my credit and financial future for t-shirts and candy bars.

My mother was right; I should have paid my tithes and built up my savings instead of chasing a trend that would be forgotten by the time I had accumulated enough savings to make a purchase. My mother had learned this from her grandmother and tried to pass on the information, but I wasn't ready. By the time I was able to appreciate the advice she had given me as a teenager, I had already passed up yet another savings opportunity (mutual funds) and had placed sizable balances on my credit cards. The next years were rough, with financial hurdles getting in the way and innumerable collection calls littering my phone line.

If, walking through the woods with your family, you tripped and fell into a hole, wouldn't you let your family know to watch out so that they don't repeat your mistake? This section works in much the same way; I have gone through the holes and sprained my ankle and am now offering you the benefit of learning from my ignorance.

Please don't make the same mistakes that I made. My mother is a wise woman; even today, as she struggles to make ends meet, she accumulates money in her accounts for a rainy day. As I mentioned, my great-grandmother, who had gone through the Great Depression, had passed on timeless information about money to my mother and saw how the family needed to have something in case of disaster. She has not been broke since. What can we learn from these women?

First, we must learn that having some savings, no matter how small, is a requirement, better yet a necessity! I meet many people who say that they cannot afford to save, but as I always ask, how can you afford not to? With two recessions in the last ten years, a national savings rate of less than zero, and an unemployment rate rapidly approaching 20%, how can you afford *not* to put any of your income back in case you lose your job or someone gets ill? And just how much should you save?

Let's set a guideline of 10% of your income. Ten percent of your income equates to $10 for every $100 that you earn. This 10% will be placed in an account without checks and without debit cards so that you cannot access the money at a moment's notice—sorry, no surprise trips to the store after a hard day at work.

Paycheck after paycheck, these funds will be deposited and forgotten as if you had never received them in the first place. Moreover, I suggest that you open up the account at a financial institution that you do not currently bank with. By doing so, you further eliminate the temptation to access the funds for everyday wants and desires.

Let's make this savings task easier for you to handle; go to your human resources department and have the 10% deposited directly into your new account. By doing so, you never see the money and will therefore never miss it. After a few months, you will not even realize that the funds are gone. Before you know it, you will, however, notice how fast savings can accumulate if you are adding to them on a consistent basis.

At some point in the future, your savings will begin to reach a sizable level and you will no longer find the savings account at your local bank to be useful. Most of these accounts pay less than 1% annually in interest. You will need additional places to put your funds so that you can earn additional interest.

Funds in **savings accounts** are pooled with the investments of the bank's reserves to earn interest. This interest income mainly benefits the bank, but since they used some of your funds in the process, you receive a nominal amount of interest.

The interest in a regular savings account is small because the capital is safe. The risk of default is extremely low, so the level of reward is also. At the end of 2009, a well-known bank paid 0.01% annually on its regular savings account while a competitor paid 0.05% annually on its regular savings accounts.

A **certificate of deposit**, or **CD**, is a second option that is available at your local bank for earning additional interest while also maintaining the safety of your principal. Your funds are deposited for a specified period of time, such as six months, one year, three years, or five years. Your access to the funds is extremely limited, under penalty of loss of the principal, in exchange for a predetermined level of interest. This interest is typically higher than the normal savings rate of interest.

Your principal is returned and your interest is paid to you at the end of the term. In the meantime, the bank can use your funds for its day-to-day lending operations.

Currently, those same national banks are offering special interest rates on their CDs, in the amount of 0.5% to 3% annually, and 0.4% to 1.9% annually, respectively, with terms ranging from nine months to five years. They both have minimums that must be deposited to achieve these rates.

Money market accounts are another option for savings at your local bank. These accounts feature higher interest rates, like CDs, but are a lot less stringent in their requirements; you have access to the funds in your money market account, but you are limited in the number of transactions that you can make per month.

If you agree to allow the bank to use your funds for lending purposes, you have the option of having your funds earn a higher percentage of interest. Most people do agree to this because they will earn extra money for something they were going to do in the first place. Furthermore, people like that their money is not tied up for long period of time in money market accounts like it is in CDs. The tradeoff for access to your funds at those same two national banks is, respectively, 0.02% and 0.15% annually, with additional accounts needed at the banks.

If you have large amounts to deposit, bankers will be more than happy to design a plan to help you earn the best available rate.

Most banks have also now expanded to include investment divisions, which allow banks to compete with brokerages in offering investment products. These investment products provide additional options for creating income from your savings and will be discussed in subsequent chapters.

As we wrap up this chapter on savings accounts, it is important to remember that savings at your local bank are insured by the Federal Deposit Insurance Corporation, or FDIC, which protects each account up to $100,000 and each depositor up to $250,000 altogether. The FDIC is charged by the federal government to maintain sound conditions in the banking system. In the event of a bank failure, the FDIC steps in to return the deposits of the accountholders who were affected, up to the account limits. This safety allows accountholders to sleep comfortably at night.

Please note that banks are marketplaces for lending and borrowing, and that your funds will be used for those purposes. It is, however, important to recognize that not all banks are created equal, and because of this inequality, neither are their payouts. The rates quoted previously from the two large banks are evidence that payouts vary widely from institution to institution.

Take your time and shop around until you find a bank that will work for you. Be sure, also, to weigh in the customer service that you receive when making your final selection. Do some research and then decide where you will place your funds. You have only so much to put away; your money should be earning top dollar while the banks have it in use. Don't let loyalty to one bank stunt your income potential!

I would also caution you not to get so wrapped up in a bank that you allow your bank to begin to offer you bad service. Do not be afraid to shop around. Remember, bankers are working for *you*. You do have a choice in where you place your money.

I once again ask that you take just ten cents from every dollar that you earn and place it in an account that is reserved solely for the "what ifs" that arise when you least expect them.

If you do this, your reliance on credit will diminish and your happiness and ultimately your health will improve. If you are still reluctant or if you feel that after doing all the exercises in this book that you cannot put away the 10% that I am suggesting, my question is, how much *can* you save? Any amount is better than zero. Make a decision and get started!

Unit 5: Investments

16

Investment Basics

Okay, so you've decided to invest. You have heard enough from your friends and coworkers about how they are making a killing in the stock market. You finally are ready to take the plunge and become an investor. Getting started is the only thing left to do. This is about the time that you realize the difficulty of the task ahead. Where do you begin?

Investing can be very complicated and intimidating. There are many terms to know and many rules to follow. Media sources, such as television and newspapers, do not readily include the basics that will give the true beginner a working knowledge of what they need to know. Unfortunately, some of investment information will be learned on the fly while you are actively involved.

If you work at a corporation, you probably have access to some forms of investment. The most common type your employer may offer is the 401(k) plan. In your 401(k), you will probably notice stock or mutual fund holdings that you have been purchasing since you signed up. Some people just sign up and never look any further because they don't understand how the plans work, while others actively manage their accounts. Since guidance is not readily available, your 401(k) is mainly self-operated. You are responsible for the gains and losses that you incur.

Investing is different than savings because you can lose money with an investment. Your funds are not guaranteed or protected from loss. You are speculating by investing, and while most have profited from their ventures into the stock markets, some have lost everything. Before you set out to fend for yourself, allow me to introduce you to some investing basics.

Stocks

You have probably heard about the stock market. Most of what you've probably heard regards its ups and downs. But what is a stock? According to MerriamWebster.com, a **stock** is the proprietorship element in a corporation, usually divided into shares and represented by transferable certificates.

When a company decides to expand past the realm of private ownership, its management has the option to solicit owners for the company to raise capital. During its incorporation, the price of a share of stock is originally set out at a par value. When the corporation goes public, its owners set an original selling price based on what they believe one share of their company is worth.

Once the selling price is determined and the legal work is complete, the company begins to trade on the stock exchanges. The corporation is now considered to be a public entity. The value of a share of the corporation is now determined by the performance of the company and by the investors who are willing to pay for ownership in the corporation.

The stock market is simply what it sounds like—a place where buyers and sellers are put together to facilitate the transfer of ownership, or stock, of the member companies listed on the exchange. By purchasing a share of a corporation's stock, you become part owner of the company. If the corporation has 100,000 shares of stock, and you purchase 1,000 shares, then you own 1/100 of the corporation. You have rights associated with being an owner. As a shareholder, you can review the company's financials. You can vote for leadership in the corporation (one share equals one vote at shareholder meetings). You share in the corporation's profits, and thus losses. You even share in the corporation's successes, or ultimately, its failures. You will maintain all of these rights until such a time that you sell your shares of stock to another investor.

You receive the aforementioned rights and the corporation receives your money to help in the day-to-day operations of the corporation. If your 1,000 shares of stock cost $20 each, then the corporation gets $20,000 (less fees) that it can use for expansion. As the corporation's performance varies, so will the corporation's stock price. If the company has an outstanding period, investors will flock to the corporation and therefore drive the cost of ownership higher. If the company performs poorly or has a lackluster period, investors will run from the corporation and the price of the stock will fall.

Ideally, the stock price would be solely dependent on the company's performance, but in reality, the price will depend on how well related companies and the overall stock market do, and on the economic outlook of the country. All of these reasons play a role in the stock price of a corporation.

Corporations that are doing well may share the profits that the company has earned with shareholders by issuing dividends. Not all companies pay out dividends; others choose to allocate these funds to expansion, research, or development. The frequency of the dividend is determined by the company's board of directors and may be paid out monthly, quarterly, or annually. At times, you may hear of a corporation skipping a dividend payout or not declaring one for a certain period, but most pay with predictable frequency once they choose to do so.

As more and more investors purchase shares of a company's stock, the company will issue more shares. This influx of investors causes the value of shares to become diluted. One way that a corporation's shares become diluted is through stock splits. For example, one share might become two, three, four, or five shares of stock. The share price would then be divided by two, three, four, or five, which means investors don't gain anything. The number of outstanding shares increases and the price of the shares go down while the value stays the same.

If the corporation feels that their shares are too diluted for the value they are receiving, they may do a **reverse split**, the opposite of what we just discussed. Five shares, four shares, three shares, or two shares become one and the share price is multiplied by that number to keep the value the same.

Conversely, if the corporation is doing well enough, some companies will choose to do a stock buyback, in which the corporation uses some of its reserve funds to buy stock directly from the investor. Many companies chose to do this after the recession between 2000 and 2009.

Any of these manipulations in stock prices are already reflected in the stock's share price on the day that they occur, so then is not necessarily the best time to invest. Do your research and invest in companies with sound management and financial results and in products that you yourself believe in. Never buy shares of a corporation just because you believe that the price of the stock is due to jump. Yes, it is great when the share prices rise quickly, but be prepared to hold onto your shares in case you get stuck for the long term.

Stock Exchanges

A stock exchange, or stock market, brings investors together to buy and sell shares of a corporation.

The **New York Stock Exchange**, or **NYSE**, is a physical marketplace for buyers and sellers to meet. You personally will not go to the NYSE, but your broker-dealer's representatives are on the trading floor. The representatives match up orders for those wishing to buy with those wishing to sell company stock. The NYSE operates as a sort of auction. You typically see the stock exchange on your local news channels when a new company is making waves or when something big takes place in the world of investing.

The **National Association of Securities Dealers Automated Quotation**, or **NASDAQ**, is an electronic rather than physical exchange. Broker-dealers list what they are willing to buy or sell a security for and the quantity of shares they have. Buyers and sellers place their order with the dealer at the price that fits their needs. As an individual investor, the process is quick and you see nothing but your order being filled and the update appearing in your account.

The **Chicago Board Options Exchange**, or **CBOE**, is a marketplace for the trading of options associated with a corporation's stock. **Options** are rights to buy or sell shares of a particular stock at a specified price. These contracts are bought and sold on an open market. Options are very advanced and outside the scope of this text.

Indexes

Among other terms that you may hear or see in various media outlets are **indexes**. These are lists of publicly traded companies and their stock prices. The companies listed are grouped by a particular method and tracked together. Some people use these indexes as a measuring stick to tell how well the economy is doing.

The **Dow Jones Industrial Average** measures the stock performance of thirty leading blue-chip United States companies and can be found at *http://www.djindexes.com*.

The **Standard and Poor's 500** index measures the stock performance of 500 large-cap stocks in the United States and can be found at *http://www.standardandpoors.com*.

There are many other indexes available for the investor to review, track, or measure their performance against. The two indexes listed above are often referenced during news broadcasts.

Additionally, the NYSE and the NASDAQ are also tracked as a whole, much like the indexes listed above.

Bonds

In the previous section, you learned that buying stock in a company entitles you to ownership rights of the corporation. As with ownership of anything, the possibility of failure or loss is always present. In fact, the common shareholders, as we have discussed in this text, are the last to be paid in the event of a company failure. This is because you cannot have the owners taking out their shares before the corporation settles the accounts of their stakeholders.

One set of stakeholders to a corporation would be bond-holders. When a corporation or government entity wants to expand or move into a different area and needs to generate some cash quickly, they can issue bonds. **Bonds** are promises to pay issued by these entities.

Imagine that your local school board would like to build a new school and raising taxes is not an option. The school board would likely schedule a special election, and if approved, would issue a set of bonds to help cover the expenses of the project. Bond elections are typically approved for school boards and allow schools to continue to provide quality education for children.

Bonds are issued with a **maturity date**, the date when the debt is to be repaid; a **coupon rate**, the amount of interest that is being paid on the debt; and a **par value**, the original value of the bond.

For instance, a bond may be issued with a ten-year, 6% coupon valued at $1000 originally. Purchasers of the bond would receive two payments a year in the amount of 3% ($30 in this case) for the next ten years, at which time the debt would be repaid in exchange for the initial investment of $1000.

Entities also have the option of making the bonds **callable**, which means that at any time, the issuer can repay the debt early in full if they have the funds available to do so. Most government bonds are callable and typically last for longer than ten years. If you see these bonds with a thirty year note, make the proper adjustment to the number of payments.

Typically, callable bonds are not just purchased and placed on a shelf; instead, they are usually traded on the open market because the value of the bonds can fluctuate. The intrinsic qualities do not change, but the selling value does change. If the par value is $1000, the bond could be selling at a premium, which means that the purchase price would be above $1000 if you wanted to buy the bond.

On the other hand, the bond could be trading at a discount, which means that the purchase price would be less than $1000. The new owner takes over receipt of the bond's interest payments at the purchase date. The previous owner receives the amount of interest from the last interest disbursement up until the purchase date.

The issuing of corporate bonds works similarly, except that government bonds receive special tax treatment. Depending on who issues them and in which state the issuer is located, some government bonds, called **municipal bonds** or **"munis"** for short, have some level of tax exemption. Corporate bonds, however, do not receive such favorable tax treatment.

Corporate bondholders are paid before the common corporate shareholders in the event that the company fails, because the bondholders are creditors of the company. In the event that the company goes under, the common shareholders get paid off if there is anything left after the creditors have settled all of their accounts. Such is the risk of being a shareholder—you can make big profits, but your capital is at risk.

Bonds are popular because they are typically more secure and a lot less risky. Purchasers of bonds would include corporations, government agencies, pension administrators, insurance agencies, banks, investment firms, and individual investors.

In the previous example, I mentioned a bond with a ten-year maturity, 6% coupon at $1000 par (original) value. Notice that the amount of interest paid on this bond is $30 every six months for the next ten years. Most of us would not get excited by this amount when it comes to just one bond. But if you multiply that number by ten or one hundred or one thousand bonds, you can see how the interest payments would begin to add up.

For a person who is looking for some security and safety, the additional income can come in handy. Did I mention that at the end of the ten years you get your money back, in this case the original $1000?

Maybe now you are getting a bit more excited. That $1000 has been gone for so long, you probably have forgotten about it, so why not do it all over again and maybe find a bond with an 8% coupon? The major risk that you face with bonds is inflation. The value of the payments can be eroded during years of high inflation, therefore limiting your purchasing power.

Some bonds are purchased at a discount and mature to their par value. Some US Treasury bonds are purchased at fifty cents on the dollar and will be worth their face value at maturity. For example, you can purchase a Series EE bond valued at $50 for $25 with a thirty year maturity. Visit *http://www.treasurydirect.gov* for more information about US savings bonds. Unlike other bonds, these bonds do not pay separate interest payments. The purchaser receives the full value at maturity after paying half for the cost of the bond. In the event that the purchaser has to relinquish the bond early, the value received as reimbursement will be adjusted.

Bonds can be a powerful addition to any investment portfolio. Your understanding of how they work and what you are entitled to is your first step in becoming an educated investor.

Mutual Funds

Now that you know what a bond is and are more aware of what stocks are, we can move to another form of investment, mutual funds. Mutual funds are very popular and are simple to purchase. How these products work is a little more complicated.

If having someone:

- choose your investments
- manage your account
- update your gains and losses
- sell stocks that are underperforming
- buy stocks that they think are due to increase in value
- spread your funds over multiple investments, and
- send you quarterly reports regarding your account

sounds good to you, then mutual funds may be for you. These accounts are professionally managed and operate within certain rules and guidelines to achieve an investment objective. **Mutual**

funds are shared investments that include resources pooled from multiple investors. The investors all contribute to the fund and share in the gains and losses of the fund. Your portion of the gains or losses will be directly related to your percentage of the total amount invested.

Mutual funds allow you to purchase shares of stock from multiple companies, often with very small amounts of money. You are able to purchase percentages of shares of stock and to build a portfolio of one hundred to three hundred fifty company stocks for as little at $50 per month. The minimums vary from mutual fund company to mutual fund company, but there are some options out there for the very small investor.

Purchasing shares of a mutual fund also spreads your possible losses across the entire portfolio instead of taking a hit by purchasing just one stock. If you were to purchase shares of one company and that one company fails, then you would lose your investment. On the other hand, if your investment is spread between a hundred companies and one company fails, you only lose the portion that is invested in that one company. Your losses are minimized in this case.

Of course, the opposite is also true; if that one company does well, then your gains are only equal to the portion that is invested in that one company. Your hope is that most of the companies do well and that as a result, you will do well.

You do have to pay for the management of the mutual funds, its advertising and marketing costs, and legal costs. These costs are passed on to you in terms of fees and charges. The advertising and marketing costs are called **12b-1 fees** and are typically listed as a percentage of the assets under management of the account and are usually charged annually. The other charges are called loads and vary from fund share class to fund share class.

The first share class is an **A share**, which includes a fee that you would pay upfront when you make a purchase in the mutual fund. When you sell your shares in the funds, you pay no fees and all of the money in the account is yours, no matter how much you have earned in the account.

The second share class is called a **B share**, which includes a fee that you would pay when you sell your shares in the fund. These shares do not charge you initially to make a purchase, but do rely on 12b-1 fees for their marketing and advertising. When you sell your shares, you are charged a fee based on how long you had the funds in the account. This fee is called a **contingent deferred sales charge**, or **CDSC**, and typically lasts up to ten years.

The third share class is called a **C share**, which has neither an upfront charge nor a CDSC. This share class instead relies on internal fees to cover its expenses. These fees are more than the internal fees in the A and B share classes. These C share funds also typically have a 12b-1 fee associated with them.

There are other share classes, but they are referenced by different letters by each fund family. Most of the other shares are reserved for retirement accounts and institutional investors.

Each mutual fund company may have one hundred or even three hundred mutual funds that they have created, all with different investment objectives. Some of the funds have a single fund manager, while others may have a committee of fund managers making investment decisions. The main goal is to profitably invest clients' funds and draw more assets under management. When a fund manager is successful, the influx of money can be overwhelming, and will cause the manager to close the fund to new investors. Once this happens, if you are already an investor in the fund, you can continue to contribute, but all others are locked out. If you leave at this point, you cannot get back in.

Some mutual funds manage millions of dollars, while others manage billions. All of the information that you would need to make a prudent investment decision is detailed in a document called a **prospectus**. Each fund company issues a prospectus for each fund that they offer.

The fund's investment objective, investment holdings, fund manager, fees, share classes, and all legal information are contained in the prospectus. Most of these prospectuses are updated annually. If there is a need for an addendum, the fund manager usually will send it to all shareholders and also post the information on their website.

Mutual funds may contain securities such as corporate stocks, corporate bonds, government bonds, real estate investments, and even loans. It is important to review the prospectus to determine whether or not an investment is suitable for you.

With mutual funds, if you can open an account, you can invest, no matter how small of an investor you may be.

Tickers

There are too many companies, too many bonds, and too many mutual funds to reference each of them by name, so they are all referenced by initials, called **ticker symbols**. Each of them has a specific reference and meaning, which makes them easy to find and to reference. Ticker symbols vary based on the type of investment that each represents.

Stocks listed on the NYSE typically have a ticker of three letters or fewer, while stocks listed on the NASDAQ typically have four symbols. Stocks not listed on an exchange but still traded are listed on what are called **pink sheets** and carry a five-symbol ticker. The availability of stock on the pink sheets is relatively low and news is typically hard to find. Use extreme caution when considering these stocks. Most have some sort of regulatory issue associated with them that prohibits them from being listed.

Stocks are actively traded throughout the day, thanks to world markets, but in the United States the markets are open between 9:30 a.m. and 4:00 p.m. (EST). If you are not in the eastern time zone, then adjust these times for your time zone. Stock prices fluctuate throughout the day during open trading hours.

Mutual funds typically have a five-letter ticker. Share classes are generally noted by a subtle change in one letter of the ticker symbol. While you can purchase shares of mutual funds at any time, most only adjust their prices and place orders based on the price as of the close of the business trading day. Mutual fund prices therefore only vary day to day.

You can reference a company's ticker symbol online via quoting sites, or in the business pages of the newspaper. There you will find opening and closing prices, the volume of shares moved, as well as the changes from yesterday's closing prices.

You will also find various charts and tables that rank the funds and the companies as top gainers, top losers, or top ten or twenty in a particular category. Some pages will have companies that are declaring dividends for the first time. You may also find information about upcoming dividends from companies that you are familiar with. If you do not know what the companies' ticker symbols are, you won't know what you are looking at.

Visit some online sites and review the ticker symbols of the companies that you purchase from regularly. Refer to your 401(k) statement and use the ticker symbols of the investments that you have in order to find information about the investment regarding performance, investment objective, and recent filings.

17

Asset Allocation

Hopefully the fog is lifting in your mind regarding investments. In the last chapter we discussed a lot of terms that you will encounter frequently when it comes to investing. Now I would like to discuss what are called asset classes.

Similar investments are grouped into categories called **asset classes**. These classes are used by investors to choose investments, to monitor specific industries, and to track performance from different countries. While there are many asset classes in existence, we will focus on a few of the most popular.

Before we discuss the asset classes in detail, let's go over a couple of terms that you should be familiar with. **Market capitalization** is the market value of a company's outstanding shares and is determined by multiplying the company's share price with the number of outstanding shares. Market capitalization is used as a dividing line for many of the asset classes that we will discuss. For example, Wal-Mart (WMT) has 3.877 billion shares outstanding and is trading at above $54 per share. By multiplying those two numbers together results in a market capitalization of over $209 billion, therefore making Wal-Mart a large-cap company.

Large-cap stocks or **large market capitalization companies** have a market capitalization of over $10 billion. These are typically the big name companies that you can easily recognize, like Wal-Mart, Exxon, and Microsoft. Large-cap companies are generally considered to be the most stable and the least risky of the asset classes.

Mid-cap stocks have a market capitalization between $2 billion and $10 billion. These companies include Belo, W. R. Grace, Del Monte, and Cintas. Mid-cap stocks fall in between the small companies and the large companies.

Small-cap stocks have a market capitalization between $300 million and $2 billion dollars. Examples of small-cap stocks are Buffalo Wild Wings, Ethan Allen Interiors, and Independent Bank. Small-cap stocks are generally considered to be riskier than both the large- and the mid-cap stocks because of their size.

International stocks are considered another asset class because they are located outside of the United States. Many of the telecommunication companies are located outside of the United States, along with some of the automakers.

Emerging markets are stocks from developing countries that are experiencing a growth explosion. Africa, South America, and some Asian countries are considered emerging markets.

Stocks from companies that are classified as small-cap, international, or emerging markets typically have greater risk than large company stocks. These stocks are typically volatile, but can produce large returns. Of course, they may also produce large negative returns as well.

Treasuries include US government-issued securities and are considered very stable. This asset class is heavily used to add safety to a portfolio.

Bonds are listed as their own asset class but are broken down into **high-yield**, **junk**, or **stable classes**. All of these produce different levels of returns and carry their own measure of risks.

There are many other asset classes available for you to review. As we continue in this chapter, we will use these asset classes along with other related terms to determine your asset allocation.

Growth vs. Value

Each stock that we discussed typically falls into one of two categories—growth stocks or value stocks. There has long been an argument as to which is better, but both have their place in a properly designed portfolio.

When companies spend most of their resources trying to improve their market capitalization by investing excess funds into expansion, research, and development, and other internal factors, they are classified as **growth stocks**. These companies rarely pay dividends and usually have very optimistic outlooks for their growth potentials.

On the other hand, when companies choose to share their profits with the shareholders in addition to internal expansion needs, they are considered to be **value stocks**. These companies issue dividends regularly and are considered to be very stable.

Growth stocks and value stocks both experience the same volatility that the rest of the market does, but typically at different times. If you were to do some research on which had the most positive periods, you would discover that both have had their years of success. You would also discover that they both have had their years of failure as well. The key to being a successful investor is to work on what is called diversification.

Similar to not putting all your eggs in one basket, **diversification** is used to lower your overall risk by spreading out your investments over many different asset classes. If one asset class is not doing well, the others can experience success and your overall portfolio can continue to gain value. Your large-cap companies can add stability to your stock portfolio, while your small-cap companies can add their ability to produce large returns. Your value investments can produce income in years when your growth investments are experiencing a decline. Your bond investments can protect your entire portfolio when the entire stock market experiences a long decline. All of these factors play a role in having a properly diversified portfolio. What you have to determine for yourself is which asset classes make you feel the most comfortable.

Can you handle the large swings of international stocks, which can vary 30% from year to year? Can you accept investing in value stocks for the income, but feel uncomfortable in not having "out of the park" gains? How much of your money are you willing to risk losing while attempting to triumph investing in the stock market? Only after you answer these questions can you design a portfolio that will produce long-term gains for you.

Market Risk

We have spent a lot of time talking about asset classes and diversification and why they are important. The major reason why having a properly designed portfolio is important is that you do experience what is called **market risk**.

The stock market is very volatile and operates like no other system on the planet. It is unpredictable in the results that it produces mainly because of one factor that cannot be controlled. This factor is human interference, namely human emotion.

The stock market, for all of the research factors, formulas, charts, trends, and education that we possess, is ultimately ruled by the emotion of the investor. If a company's share price is increasing dramatically, then everyone wants to get in on the gains. When that company's share price becomes too expensive, investors turn to the competitors in the same industry and drive their prices up too. These competing companies are inflated simply by being in the same industry as one another, and not for their individual performance.

What do you think happens when these competing companies post their performance numbers, such as their percentage of growth for the period and return on invested capital, and the numbers do not support the price that they have benefited by having? Investors will run because the companies did not meet expectations of the driven-up price. Once investors begin to run, the competitors' share prices will begin to go down as well, and the stock market has a bad day.

Weather events can cause investors to sell their shares of stock because of the possibility that a company will miss its forecast now that a hurricane, typhoon, blizzard, or drought has hit the region. This sell-off is based on panic instead of sound judgment. It is a purely emotional response, but is powerful enough to drive the stock market down by many points.

We have seen the stock market take a dip due to the election of a new president or pope, a change in the weather, a change in interest rates, a war, a shortage in one sector, a gloomy day in the city, or just because of a bad night's sleep.

If you do invest in the stock market, get ready for a lot of things to not make sense. Try to limit your emotional responses and remind yourself of why you made your purchase in the first place. By doing so, you will limit your chances of failing early and missing out on what has built many millionaires in this country.

If you record all of your trades and the reasons why you purchased them and develop an exit strategy, you can go back and reference it in the event of a steep market decline. If all of the factors that led you to place the buy order are still relevant and still meet your criteria, then you do not have to sell. Instead, being the savvy investor that you are, you can now buy new shares at a lower price.

Your exercise for this chapter is to look over your investment statements and ask yourself the following questions:

- ✓ Which asset classes am I invested in and why?
- ✓ How can I spread out some of my risks among my numerous investments and still keep the same return?
- ✓ Can I choose different investments for the same level of risk and get higher returns?
- ✓ Why did I purchase these investments?
- ✓ How much of a market decline can I withstand at any one time?
- ✓ At what point would I like to sell this investment?
- ✓ What is my exit strategy?

18

Dollar Cost Averaging

The market is falling, the market is falling, what should I do?
Run, hide, and sell—no, buy!
What, buy? Are you crazy?

Being an investor requires that you have the courage of a firefighter. That same courage that it takes to run into a building when everyone else is running out is what it will take to be a successful investor. Successful investors move in the opposite direction of the pack because they know that the pack is usually wrong.

When the market takes a turn for the worse, most investors choose to sell all that they have on the way down. Successful investors know that when the market starts to decline, opportunities are on the rise. Think of market declines as a sale that everyone is invited to. Most small investors choose to run and hide, so this sale is still a best-kept secret.

When the stock market has a major decline, we as investors are given an opportunity to make up for lost time. We can buy solid companies that are priced within our means. Often these companies were caught up in the fallout from the panic and had their prices brought to low levels. The problem for the investor is that these companies won't stay at rock-bottom prices for long.

As investors, we have to realize that we are already too late when our grandmother calls us with stock tips. We have to understand that we cannot time the market, but instead must have a solid plan that will help us to be successful. We must recognize that choosing companies without prior knowledge of their operations or just because someone else has mentioned the share price is going up is like throwing darts at a dartboard with our eyes closed. We must also understand that by the time a stock tip hits a publication or a television show, the wave has passed us by. These are mistakes that investors make all the time.

Instead of making the mistake of relying on old information and fear when choosing investments, the proper way to invest is to buy your shares at low prices and to sell them when the prices get high. At the end of the day, all that the investor should care about is the number of shares he or she owns and the share price at the time that he or she places the order to sell.

If the company that he or she purchased is solid, then there is no need to bail out. If the investor is worried about losses, then he or she can place some safety measures to limit the number of losses that he or she can incur.

The problem that investors face is the emotion behind investments. You must force yourself to follow the plan, to track your investments, to make adjustments, and to correct your mistakes. You must be willing to let go of investments for a loss sometimes so that you can replace them with more profitable investments, but you must also convince yourself to never look back with regrets about an investment decision that you made.

The market is volatile and guaranteed to go up and down. Just how far up or how far down from day to day is a mystery, but you must be aware of that fact. If you know this to be true, then you can create a system where you can take advantage of some of the changes in the market; one such system is called dollar cost averaging.

Dollar cost averaging is a systematic investment plan used by investors to take timing the market out of the investment process. Everyone knows that the market is going to go up and down daily. Dollar cost averaging investors invest the same amount of money the same day of every period. If the period is monthly, then an investor using dollar cost averaging would invest his or her money, for example, on the 1st, 10th, or 15th of every month.

By doing so, the investor will purchase fewer shares on the days when the price is high and will purchase more shares when the price is low. At the end of the day, when the investor cashes in his or her shares for money, the average cost of all of the shares will be higher than it would have been had the investor made the purchase all at once.

Timing of the market is removed from the process in dollar cost averaging, so you don't have to worry about waiting for the wave and missing out because you were at work, playing sports, or on vacation instead of watching a ticker scroll across the bottom of a screen.

View Table 7 for more details on how the process works.

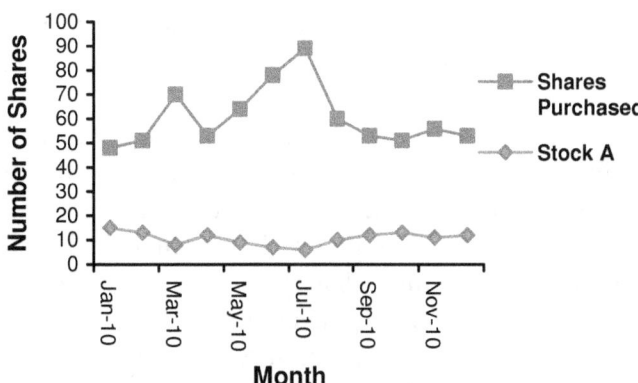

Table 7: Monthly Investment $500 Shares Purchased vs. Share Price

Table 7 shows investments made monthly in the amount of $500. If the original investment had been made in the amount of $6000 in January, the number of shares purchased would have been 400, and the average price per share would have been $15. Instead, by spreading out the purchase through the year, the investor accumulates 598 shares because he or she purchased more shares during the months that the share price declined.

Investors do not realize losses or gains until they sell the shares that they own. Assuming that this investor chose to sell at the end of the year, the ending values would be:

One-time $6000 investment: 400 shares x $12/share = $4800

vs.

Dollar cost average $500/month: 598 shares x $12/share = $7176

The average cost per share would be $10.66 and the investor would have a profit of $1176 as a result of the selection. This is a simplified example of a volatile stock, but shows how systematically spreading out your investment over time can help you to benefit from some of the downturns that the stock market takes.

Another benefit to the investor is that he or she doesn't have to actively watch the portfolio, waiting to see if the market will do what would be most beneficial.

One final benefit to dollar cost averaging versus investing a lump sum all at once is the ability to ease into the market, like a swimmer checking the temperature of the water. Most investors' greatest fear is that they will place their trade order to buy an investment and immediately watch the investment drop and keep dropping. Dollar cost averaging allows you to ease your way into the market and therefore lessen the initial shock in the event that your investment takes a nosedive as soon as you jump in.

Look at your retirement plan at work and notice that your investments typically happen the day after your receive your pay. On some pay dates you will purchase shares at a higher price and on others you will purchase on lows. Your retirement plan helps you to invest automatically every time you get paid at work.

Your investment accounts, however, are solely your responsibility if you are a self-directed investor. If you have an investment professional handling your account, contact him or her to find out if you are taking advantage of this powerful investment strategy.

It is time to take a more active role in your investment portfolio. Remember that you are the boss—take charge, ask questions, and become more informed. Lastly, don't be afraid to ask for help.

Unit 6: Charitable Contributions

19

Tithes

I am including this chapter because, for many people in this country, the concept of tithing is a major belief. Personally, being a Christian, I believe that tithing is still necessary in this day and age. Nestled in the book of Malachi, it is written that 10% of the harvest should be donated to the church to do the Lord's work. If you're not a Christian, I am sure there's a means whereby your place of worship generates support to perform daily business and to conduct its works. Tithing is one such method that is used to do a variety of things, including community development, assistance to the elderly, and assistance to the sick and the unemployed, as well as the other needs of the church. Your donations become the way that educational programs are funded or the means by which the troubled member can receive assistance in a time of need.

In the past, churches, rather than banks, funded loans to grow community programs. Today, churches still serve many people, especially the elderly and those in community programs. Your small contribution, pooled with the contributions of others of your faith, helps the single mother of five to cover her rent and to settle up on utility bills. These tithes help to send underprivileged youth to college, purchase school supplies, provide meals for the less fortunate, and help many with counseling services.

No matter by what name it is called, the contribution to help someone else is what being human is about. You should give freely, not worry where the funds have been placed, and recognize that the small sacrifice that you made will make a difference somewhere.

In the chapter on paying yourself first, I mentioned that for some households the amount of money available for monthly expenses would be 80%. All of us have an inherent desire to help others. We give billions of dollars annually to churches, charities, and educational institutions. Do we do so because we're forced? No, we do so because deep down we all want to make a difference. Tithing is how most of us can make a difference. On a personal note, as a child, I benefited from donations from a church that my family had just joined. Word got out that we were struggling with an out-of-work single parent and an inability to pay bills, and the church began to deliver aid to us without our request. Our utilities were paid and we received clothes and food. We were given funds to help with our monthly rent. It wasn't a lot, but it was enough to get us through a difficult time. I am sure that during our worship there, we more than repaid the church and also helped the next family by paying our tithes.

Be cheerful and give. Take note that you are helping to bring joy to someone desperately in need. You never know how much your small contribution can change the life of someone you may know or may never meet. From someone whose life was touched by donations like yours, thank you! As I was told as a child, pay it forward, keep helping others, and ours becomes a better world.

20

Charity: When a Good Deed Is Not as It Appears

Being helpful or charitable to your fellow man is very important in many religions. Many of us have done some form of charity work or made some sort of donation to a person or organization. After all, we all know someone who is less fortunate than we are, and it feels good to help someone in need. We never know if it will be our turn next.

No matter who we help, we hope that our actions will not be misused. We believe and must be assured that our donation is used for the purpose for which it was given. When we are wronged, our willingness to help others diminishes and our reluctance increases. With hardened hearts we will deny any request for aid because of our distrust.

I can recall a story that details such a betrayal of my trust that the remainder of my day was ruined. I had elected to not help anyone else because of the severity of this betrayal.

On a warm fall day I drove into a gas station to get some gasoline for a trip I was beginning. I was met by a man walking slowly behind a child. As I finished pumping my gas, the man approached me with something in his hand. I had begun to suspect that he would ask me for some spare change.

Though I usually dismiss these requests without a second thought, this time was different; the man was holding two coins in his hand and had a vehicle parked a couple of pumps away. He explained that he had run out of gas and only had fifty cents for which to purchase gas. He continued by stating that he was trying to get his son back across town to his mother and that he wanted fifty more cents so that he could buy a dollar worth of gas to accomplish the task. I explained that I did not have any change but that I would purchase him some gasoline so that he could get the child home safely.

Maybe I did it because I had run out of gas before and had been helped out by others, but mainly I think it was because I saw the little boy wandering around the parking lot. Without hesitation, I purchased the man a few dollars of gasoline. Feeling good about my deed and having watched the man proceed to pump the gas, I pulled away to leave.

But to my dismay and disgust, I observed the gentleman walking up to another customer with his hand held out and the two coins again in his hand. I clenched my jaw as he again called the little boy over to his side and once again told his story. I could not believe my eyes. Upset and feeling stupid, I drove away, adamant that I would never help anyone again.

A sense of calm came about me as I replayed the event in my mind. I had done a good deed, for which I would be rewarded later. My duty was to give cheerfully; his punishment would come about later. I would not have been so upset or considered this story worthy to tell had it not been for the child being pulled into the story. That the little boy was being used as a pawn left me with an empty feeling in my stomach. For that reason alone, I feel confident that this was one case where the need was faked.

Charity itself is never bad. Helping others is not a difficult task. For every story like mine there are many more where the need was justified. Do not let your heart harden to the point that the one time someone really needs you, you let them down.

If you give, give cheerfully. Give knowing that you will not get anything in return. Give, not expecting anything in return, not even a thank you! This is the true essence of charity.

Unit 7: Insurance

21

Auto Insurance

Auto insurance is one of those necessities that most of us purchase with anguish and lots of trepidation. Everyone knows that they need it, but no one likes that they don't use what they are paying for. Year after year, we pay premiums and at the end of the term, feel as though the money was just thrown away. Even though the small amount we paid was to cover the possibility of an accident, we feel that we should get something back. We never think about how the insurance company loses every time it has to pay a claim. Unfortunately, we pay for what we hope to never need to use.

How do you shop for auto insurance? Do you spend all day calling agents and giving out your personal information over and over again? Do you call your friends and family and ask for a recommendation? Do you try to sift through all of the useless information on the Web and try to find your quote there? Do you call your financial adviser and hope that he or she knows someone to recommend?

No matter which method you use to shop for auto insurance, most times you will still have more questions after you make the purchase than you did before you began.

How much coverage is enough? Is there such a thing as paying too much? Is there a way to purchase too much auto insurance? In the event of an accident, will state minimum coverage be sufficient to cover the damages?

We purchase auto insurance because our state requires us to. If having coverage was optional, a vast number of Americans would skip out on having it. Some of us only buy the minimum coverage as required by state law.

In Texas, the state mandated minimum coverage is $25,000, and while this may seem like a lot of money at first, the reality is that there are cars on the road today that cost three to four times that amount. Your personal finances could be in danger if you were to damage one of those vehicles in the event of an accident. This fact is often overlooked by motorists in every state around the country. Having auto insurance does not remedy our liability in the event of an accident. We can still be sued and held liable for damages in excess of the limits of our policies.

Which would you prefer, to increase your limits and pay just a little bit more to know that you are covered or to drive around and hope that when you do have an accident, the car that you hit is not a luxury vehicle?

Typically the difference in the monthly premium is only about $10 a month, but the comfort of knowing you're covered is priceless.

What about additional coverage, such as personal injury protection and uninsured motorist coverage?

Parts of an Auto Insurance Policy

Table 8 lists the minimum required coverage amounts for motorists in the respective states per their state law. Please note that these numbers do change, so contact your agent for up-to-date minimum requirements for your state. Notice that there are three different numbers for each state. Let's take a look at what each of these numbers refers to.

Alaska 50/100/25	Alabama 25/50/25	Arkansas 25/50/25	Arizona 15/30/10	California 15/30/5
Colorado 25/50/15	Connecticut 20/40/10	Delaware 15/30/10	Florida 10/20/10	Georgia 25/50/25
Hawaii 20/40/10	Idaho 20/50/15	Illinois 20/40/15	Indiana 25/50/10	Iowa 20/40/15
Kansas 25/50/10	Kentucky 25/50/10	Louisiana 15/30/25	Maine 50/100/25	Maryland 20/40/15
Massachusetts 20/40/5	Michigan 20/40/10	Minnesota 30/60/10	Mississippi 25/50/25	Missouri 25/50/10
Montana 25/50/10	Nebraska 25/50/25	New Hampshire 25/50/25	New Jersey 15/30/5	New Mexico 25/50/10
Nevada 15/30/10	New York 25/50/10	North Carolina 30/60/25	North Dakota 25/50/25	Ohio 12.5/25/7.5
Oklahoma 25/50/25	Oregon 25/50/10	Pennsylvania 15/30/5	Rhode Island 25/50/25	South Carolina 25/50/25
South Dakota 25/50/25	Tennessee 25/50/15	Texas 25/50/25	Utah 25/65/15	Virginia 25/50/20
Vermont 25/50/10	Washington 25/50/10	Wisconsin 50/100/55	West Virginia 20/40/10	Wyoming 25/50/20

Table 8: State-Required Auto Insurance Limits

- **Liability coverage**—broken into two parts, bodily injury and property damage, liability coverage will protect the insured against claims filed against the insured or drivers of the insured's business.
  - **Bodily injury coverage** will protect against claims arising out of injuries to motorists of vehicles involved in an accident with the insured. Typically this coverage has an expressed limit per person and per accident to which the insurance

company will pay. At a minimum, motorists should carry at least a 100/300 liability limit, which means $100,000 in coverage for one person and $300,000 for all persons per accident. These represent the first two numbers in the chart above, with the first number representing the amount of coverage per person and the second representing the per-accident amount of coverage the insurer will pay.

  o **Property damage coverage** will protect the insured in the event the insured damages the property of others. Again, the limit selected for this type of coverage is dependent on the insured. I believe $100,000 in coverage to be sufficient. Consult your agent and financial adviser before making your selection. The third number in the chart above represents the amount of coverage for this particular benefit.

- **Comprehensive insurance** protects the car against non-collision damages.
- **Collision insurance** will cover the cost to repair the insured's vehicle in the event of an accident or collision with another object.
- **Uninsured or underinsured motorists coverage** will protect the insured against losses inflicted by someone who does not have insurance or does not have sufficient coverage to cover the damages.
- **Personal injury protection** covers medical expenses in the event of an accident with the insured or anyone else in the insured's car.

The 100/300/100 policy limits that you saw in this chapter are for reference only and would be considered by most to be sufficient coverage. Before making any changes to your policy, it is highly recommended that you consult your financial adviser and insurance professional.

There are other provisions to the policy. Ask your agent questions to make sure that you are informed of your rights and the policy's limitations and that your expectations match what the company has agreed to pay for in writing.

You should reevaluate your policy, your coverage amounts, and your insurer annually. Check your area for competing agents and policy items and be certain that you are getting the best product for your money. Don't just assume that you are getting the best deal because you have been with the company for a long time.

With current technology, most people do not have to physically meet up with their agents to renew their policies. The computer produces the new rates and sends out the renewal notice and you pay it and keep going on with your life. The process is even easier than that, since with automatic withdrawals from your account or credit card, you never even need to look at the cost of the new coverage.

After a while, you seldom pay attention to your slowly increasing premiums. One day when you are bored, snowed in, or just have an extra minute, you take a look at the premiums.

You then call your agent and give him or her some choice words. Still upset, you hang up the phone and begin your search for a new policy and a new agent and the process starts over again.

Take control of your finances and make sure that you are not paying too much for your auto insurance. Encourage your agent to put your renewal on his or her calendar and request a phone call to go over the policy. Some agents cover multiple carriers and may be able to keep your business by placing your coverage with one of their other highly rated companies. You don't simply have to switch agents, unless of course you don't have any other options or have found a deal that makes it worth the change.

A word of caution—do not purchase an insurance policy based solely on price. When it comes to insurance, you will get what you pay for every time. If you get four proposals and they are all within a few dollars of each other but one is half the price of the other three, then buyer, beware!

Look at each company's creditors' ratings and complaints filed against them with the state's insurance department, and evaluate their financials before you make your final decision.

Review your auto insurance policies. What limits do you have? When was the last time that you had a conversation with your auto insurance agent?

22

Life Insurance

Another method of transferring risk is by purchasing coverage on the life of an individual. Life insurance allows the insured to provide for his or her beneficiaries once the insured is deceased. College planning, income protection, debt repayment, and charitable donations are just a few examples of uses for life insurance proceeds.

While some people are able to provide for their beneficiaries using their own means, others must rely on trading premiums for the large lump sum of cash that life insurance policies provide to help them to accomplish the goals that the insured was not able to accomplish prior to his or her passing. Although death is the one certainty that we must all face, not all of us are prepared for when we depart. Careful planning, using life insurance as one of the primary vehicles, can help to bridge the gap between a lifetime of struggle and a great legacy for the insured.

The insured's ability to earn an income is his or her greatest asset, and with people depending on this ability, the need is present for the protection provided by insurance. A business may even purchase insurance on persons that the entity is greatly dependent upon and whose deaths would cause serious setbacks for the company.

Life insurance is underwritten by the insurance company, and a risk determination is provided after reviewing the insured's age, medical history, and various lifestyle factors. The younger the insured is, the less expensive the coverage will be. As the insured ages, the premiums will increase also, albeit in a nonlinear fashion.

There are two major types of life insurance policies, term and permanent. **Term life insurance** is considered temporary insurance because, as the name suggests, the coverage only exists for the "term" or period that the coverage has been purchased. At the end of the period, the policy expires and the coverage is terminated. The policy can be renewed for another term in the event that the need still exists. The insurance company will review the insured's health again and then set a premium to be locked in for the next term.

The term of the coverage varies from company to company, but most offer terms of ten, twenty, and often thirty years. Other companies feature five- and fifteen-year policies as well. The premiums are calculated for the entire term and then are broken into smaller payments. Premiums remain locked in place until the policy terminates, either by failure to make payments or by reaching the end of the period.

Another benefit of term life insurance is that the premiums are relatively low for the amount of coverage that the insured can purchase. If purchased early enough, millions of dollars of coverage can be purchased for less than a thousand dollars per year. Term life insurance has no cash value, however, which means that it has no redemption value in the event that the policy terminates prematurely. Term life insurance is often considered "pure" life insurance because of this feature.

Some companies have begun to offer term insurance that features a **"return of premium" rider** for an additional fee. In the event that the insured is still living at the end of the term, the insurance company will return the premiums paid with a small amount of interest. This allows some people to rest easier, knowing that they will receive their money back in the event that the insured's death does not occur during the term.

Most term life insurance policies also have a conversion feature, which allows the policy owner to convert the term policy to a permanent life insurance policy within a specified period of time.

The second, more complicated type of life insurance is **permanent life insurance**. This type of life insurance features a cash value component that accumulates interest over the life of the policy. Unlike term insurance, in which the premiums are calculated over the term of the policy, permanent life insurance premiums are calculated over the lifetime of the insured. In the early years, the policy accumulates additional cash value that in the later years will be used to keep the policy in force. These accumulated funds earn a small portion of interest or dividends as defined by the insurance carrier.

Permanent life insurance, or **cash value life insurance**, requires higher premiums because of the cash accumulation and also the guarantees that the policy provides. There are a few different types of permanent life insurance. I will briefly introduce the various types but will leave it to you to contact your insurance professional for the details.

The first type, **whole life insurance**, is probably the most widely used type of permanent insurance. The premiums remain level for the life of the policy. Flexibility is limited with this type of policy because of all the guarantees that the policy carries. Early versions of whole life insurance were paid out when the insured reached one hundred years of age. Newer versions have extended that date, due to the increased longevity of our population.

The second type of permanent life insurance is called **universal life insurance**, and was designed to be more flexible than whole life insurance. Universal life policies feature a target premium that must be reached annually but allows for the option of paying more or less than the target premium and still keeping the policy in force in the event that the policy owner has any financial difficulties. There is a minimum premium that must be paid to keep the policy from terminating, and a maximum limit that keeps the policy from being taxed as a modified endowment contract by the IRS. Universal life insurance accumulates cash value and pays interest on the accumulated value after certain costs are deducted. Interest rates are declared by the insurance carrier.

A third type of permanent life insurance is called **variable universal life insurance**, and features subaccounts that are invested in the financial markets. Gains and losses in the subaccounts affect the amount of cash that is available in the policy. Premiums are flexible within limits, just like in universal life policies, and they carry many of the same guarantees. Variable universal life products are considered to be securities and are overseen by FINRA, the Financial Industry Regulatory Authority. Variable universal life carriers are required to issue a prospectus detailing the subaccounts, all fees, and the manager of all investments in the plan.

Most permanent life insurance policies feature the ability of the insured to make withdrawals and also feature a loan provision for access to the accumulated cash in the policy. Some restrictions will apply to the amount and the timeframe in which the withdrawals and loans can be accessed and will be detailed in your documentation. The IRS imposes penalties if certain rules are not adhered to with regard to life insurance policies. Consult your insurance professional for the ins and outs of these policies.

Used correctly, life insurance is a powerful estate-planning tool and a great way to provide for loved ones who would miss the insured in the event of their death. Remember that life insurance is not for the benefit of the insured, but for the ones that the insured leaves behind.

23

Disability Income Insurance

As mentioned in the last chapter, your ability to earn an income is your greatest asset. Protecting that asset should be a number one priority. Most people, however, don't consider **disability income insurance** as a method of protecting the ability to earn their income.

I have run into many people selling **accident insurance**, which covers you in the event of an accident or injury and provides you with a small amount of cash to cover your expenses, but rarely does anyone offer disability income insurance unless you sit down with a financial service professional. Employers offer long-term and oftentimes short-term disability income insurance at a small cost to the employee, but many who select the coverage are unaware of what they are purchasing.

At least these employers are providing the option of protecting your income. The employer, in this case, pays the majority of the premiums, and the employee is asked to cover the remaining portion. The benefit is that the employee will receive some income in the event that he or she is unable to work.

As a population, we insure our homes, our cars, and our possessions, but rarely do we insure our bodies. We have a greater likelihood of being disabled than your DVD player has of breaking within the first two years of use. Most of us think that we are invincible, but just ask the mothers at your workplace how many of them were placed on bed rest due to complications with their pregnancies. Ask the weekend sports players how many days of work they missed for torn knees and elbows. Ask around to the number of people who broke something just doing simple household chores. Take a family history of illnesses and diseases and find out what secrets your family tree holds. The more you look around, the more you should realize that getting hurt or seriously ill to the point of being unable to work is not as uncommon as you would like to believe. According to the 1985 Exposure Draft Report of the Society of Actuaries' Committee to Recommend New Disability Tables for Valuation, before age forty, there is a 40% chance that a person will suffer a disability of 90 days or longer.

Some disabilities only affect your household for a short period of time. Once the recovery is complete, you can get back on track and continue living your life. Other disabilities derail your life financially, mentally, and physically for long periods of time. Your ability to earn an income is taken away from you. You are forced to accept government or family aid, to become a burden at a time when you feel you should be able to provide for yourself. Your retirement accounts are halted, your medical bills increase, and your mental state begins to deteriorate with some of the longer-lingering disabilities. Even your ability to provide for your children can be affected.

While insurance companies know for a fact that you will die at some point, they are not as sure when it comes to your experiencing a disability, so they therefore underwrite the policies differently. The underwriting for the disability income insurance is more stringent and often more detailed. Most of the companies want to eliminate classes of people who have an extremely high chance of becoming disabled. People with dangerous vocations, high-risk recreational activities, and long histories of illnesses are the first to be declined for coverage. Disability insurers will offer coverage that can equal up to 70% or 80% of a person's after-tax income to those individuals who fall within their guidelines.

Payments received from disability income policies can be used to cover mortgages, rent, utilities, food, health needs, and so on. While you are recovering from your illness, injury or disability, you can still receive a monthly income. Some policies will even continue to contribute to your retirement plans so that you can still enjoy a retirement after your disability.

Disability Income Insurance

Coverage amounts vary from vocation to vocation. The length of time the insured can receive payments varies also. Most companies offer six-month, one-year, two-year, five-year, ten-year, and to-age-65 benefit periods. The insured, if disabled, would receive payments according to his or her policy up to the length of the benefit period. Some vocations do not qualify for the longer benefit periods, so consult your insurance professional regarding your specific vocation.

If the disability income plan is an individual policy and not one set up by an employer, the insured will have the option of selecting his or her waiting period. Typical waiting periods, or **elimination periods**, can range from thirty days up to one year. These will vary from company to company. During the elimination period, benefits are not paid and the insured must rely on his or her own resources for survival. Some carriers will retroactively pay for the elimination period after the disability has continued for a specific length of time.

Disability income insurance policies also include other features and provisions that I won't discuss here. You should review all of these features before you make a purchasing decision. Remember that the better the benefit, the shorter the waiting period, and the more perks you put into the plan, the greater the modal premium will be.

Disability income insurance also allows you to protect your income as earned by your profession. The protection is called "own occupation," and unlike Social Security, where your disability is deemed to be valid if you cannot perform any profession, the **"own occupation" protection** allows the insured to receive payments as long as he or she cannot perform any of the duties of his or her occupation. For example, a surgeon who can no longer perform the duties of a surgeon but can teach can still qualify for some benefits. Disability income insurance carriers only require that your doctor certify the disability before you qualify for benefits. There is no need to see a doctor of the carrier's choosing.

If you are self-employed or a business owner, you too have options when it comes to disability income protection. Your options not only extend to protecting yourself, but can also protect your business in the event that one of your key employees has a disability that removes him or her from your workplace. Again, the details are outside of the scope of this book, but they should be reviewed the next time you consult with your insurance professional.

Ask yourself the following questions:

- ✓ In the event that I became hurt or disabled, could my family or household survive without my income?
- ✓ How long could my savings last in the event that I was no longer able to work?
- ✓ If I lost my job, would my disability income benefits continue?
- ✓ Do I need disability income insurance?

Sum It All Up

I hope that you have learned a lot by reading this book. You should now be able to evaluate your financial life by taking a look at your finances from many different perspectives. I leave you with one last set of tips regarding cost-cutting measures.

Here are some additional ways to save money on a monthly basis:

1. Don't spend change from dollar bills—place your coins in a pail, bucket, or bag and cash them in when the container is full.
2. Pack a lunch once more per week instead of eating out. This can save you $500 per year just by brown-bagging it once per week.
3. Buy snacks in bulk and carry them to school or work. Items in vending machines are overpriced. You probably noticed that you spent a lot in this area when you did the tracking exercise.
4. Eat at home one more time per week. Depending on your household size, this is clearly a savings of $10–$50 per week.
5. Close all department store accounts. The interest is too high and the benefit is not worth the cost. The convenience is also too dangerous.
6. Install ceiling fans to conserve cooling costs in the summer.

7. Lower your thermostat by one degree to save on heating costs in the winter.
8. Use coupons. Take advantage of doubling and tripling them at your local merchants. Visit sites such as *http://www.grocerygame.com* for help in shopping with coupons.
9. Buy a metal coffee filter and a programmable coffee pot and lose the $4 cups of coffee.
10. Contribute up to your company match in your retirement accounts.
11. Put back two items that you don't need when you get to the checkout at the grocery store.
12. Read about, talk about, and treat your money like it is—a rare resource that you have limited amounts of.

Your financial toolbox is full! Now get to work, revisit the book six months from now, and check your progress.

So how did you do? Did you make it through in the twenty-eight days?

Remember, you don't need a winning lottery ticket to get where you would like to be financially; you just need smart choices and a commitment to excel past your current limits, to broaden your horizons, and to ask for help.

If it takes you longer than twenty-eight days, then don't give up. If you make mistakes, correct them and try again. The point of it all is for you to take command of your finances.

Look at your money through different lenses and choose to become active in the management of all of your financial affairs.

The first step is the biggest step. Good luck and God bless!

www.ingramcontent.com/pod-product-compliance
Lightning Source LLC
Chambersburg PA
CBHW051531170526
45165CB00002B/690